I0483477

LOCAL COLORING

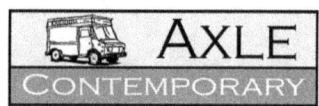

Axle Contemporary
P.O. Box 22095
Santa Fe, New Mexico 87502
www.axleart.com

Axle Contemporary would like to thank all the talented
writers and artists that contributed to the realization of this
book.

LOCAL COLORING is made possible with the support of
Axle Projects, Inc. which is generously supported by grants
from the City of Santa Fe's 1% Lodger's Tax, The McCune
Charitable Foundation, and New Mexico Arts, a division
of the Department of Cultural Affairs and the National
Endowment for the Arts.

©2017 Axle Contemporary
Stories © Melody Sumner Carnahan, Jamie Figueroa, Nasario García,
Joe Hayes, Lily Hoang
Drawings © the individual artists
All rights reserved.

ISBN: 978-0-9963991-2-8
No part of the book may be used or reproduced without permission from the publisher.

Front cover: detail, Rose Simpson
Back cover: detail, Erika Wanenmacher

LOCAL COLORING

5 Writers
67 Artists

Axle Contemporary Press

At Axle Contemporary, our goal has always been to exhibit art to our community, from our community, in unique ways. The book you are holding now is the result of one of these efforts.

We contacted five New Mexico-based creative writers, and asked each one to compose a short, image-rich story for the project. What resulted are wonderful stories with a variety of styles and cultural references, both local and universal. Figueroa and Hoang bring us fantastical images of giants and monsters. García pulls us into old-time small-town Norteño fiestas and dark back roads imbued with mystery and magic. Hayes shoots us to the stars and back with a coyote tale, and Carnahan spins us in circles (while reminding us to keep breathing) with a dizzying array of imagery.

When the stories were complete, we invited a group of artists, known for their drawing ability, to make coloring book style line drawing illustrations based on the stories. Later we had an open call to any New Mexican to contribute a drawing. Our effort culminates in an exhibition of the original drawings in the mobile gallery and this celebratory book. Feel free to grab your crayons or markers and color between the lines. Or just turn the pages and enjoy the stories and drawings all sprung forth from the imaginations of our colorful local artists.

(BREATHE)

Melody Sumner Carnahan

Four black swans float in a dark pond ( ) one white duck watches from a dry rock ledge ( ) on the birth side of the unfinished cathedral ( ) leaves turn to birds turn to stars ( ) the dressed stone glistens smelling of soap and money ( ) across the street, children pay to ride ( ) in circles ( ) in spirals ( ) with blinking lights and noise ( ) he calls out the price with a voice from hell ( ) nearby alley sells whiskey and cadavers, the caracara bird ( ) lives ( ) in the zoo, its left wing snapped ( ) crows in groups are free to come and go ( ) in the cold red light ( ) where owls and night birds hatch, a Bengali tiger roams, wearing stripes of gold and white ( ) she ( ) has ( ) the ( ) face of God ( ) the sacred Ibis repeatedly taps the ground with its beak ( ) at water's edge sunset hour patterned cast concrete pieces wash up on shore along with chunks of wood and *bomba volcanica* and fragments of steel mesh embedded in glass ( ) an unworked feldspar column divides ( ) the beach in half ( ) one side young girls practice judo kicks ( ) the other side old men in red bathing trunks swim out in high tide ( ) this winter brings the coldest air in thirty years but it makes little difference to these white-haired, ruddy chested, thin-legged men ( ) it is so dark now the boatman lights a match to read the coins I drop into his hand ( ) two heavy wood oars, a fiberglass boat, I paddle around the pond three times stopping near ( ) the duck's nest ( ) the waterfall ( ) bowing my head to glide beneath the footbridge over which roller skaters pass ( ) in the public square I'm surprised to find rope-soled persons of all ages dancing together on cobblestones while children fuel bonfires with discarded Christmas trees, broken office chairs, smashed cassette players, and plastic bags filled with data sheets ( ) they sing and clap in rhythm tossing atomizer cans into the flames, which explode to shouts of glee ( ) my mind fills with imagery from the *Museo de Arte Moderno* ( ) an engraving titled "Cupid's First Sight of Psyche" ( ) she's lying prone fair breasts exposed her head dropped back in a faint her right arm dangling in the pool into which a cascade of water falls ( ) Cupid's face is full of doom ( ) and longing ( ) he bends over her in bewilderment ( ) ( ) in the engraving titled "Cupid Reviving Psyche" she's awake and radiant, her nakedness covered, his features composed ( ) the two are depicted in a seascape with stormy clouds and the moon battling for supremacy ( ) however, the water is missing ( ) there is no water in the sea ( ) all the water in the sea has been drawn back steeply in preparation for a tidal wave.

Nina Mastrangelo

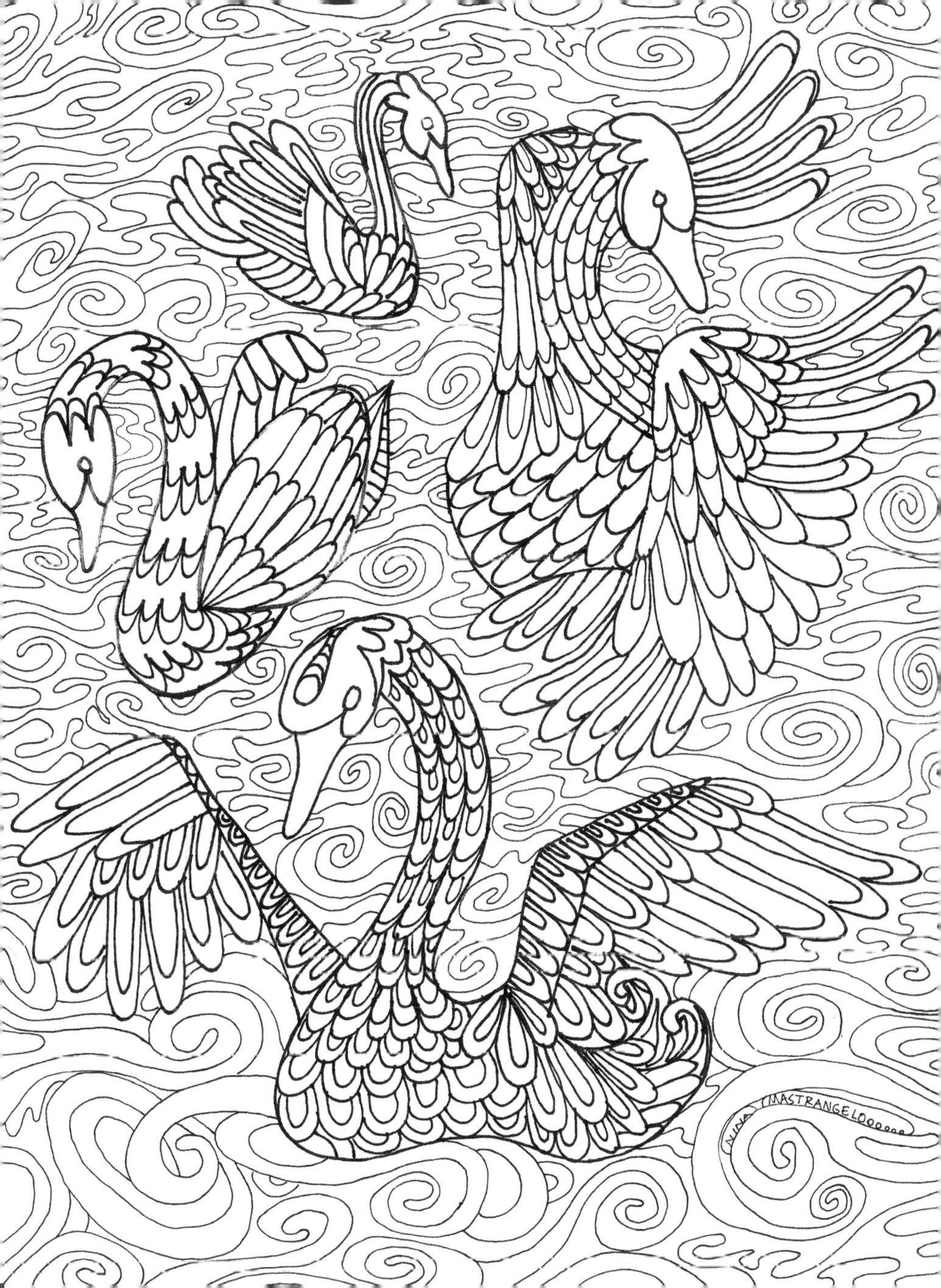

Mary Moegenberg

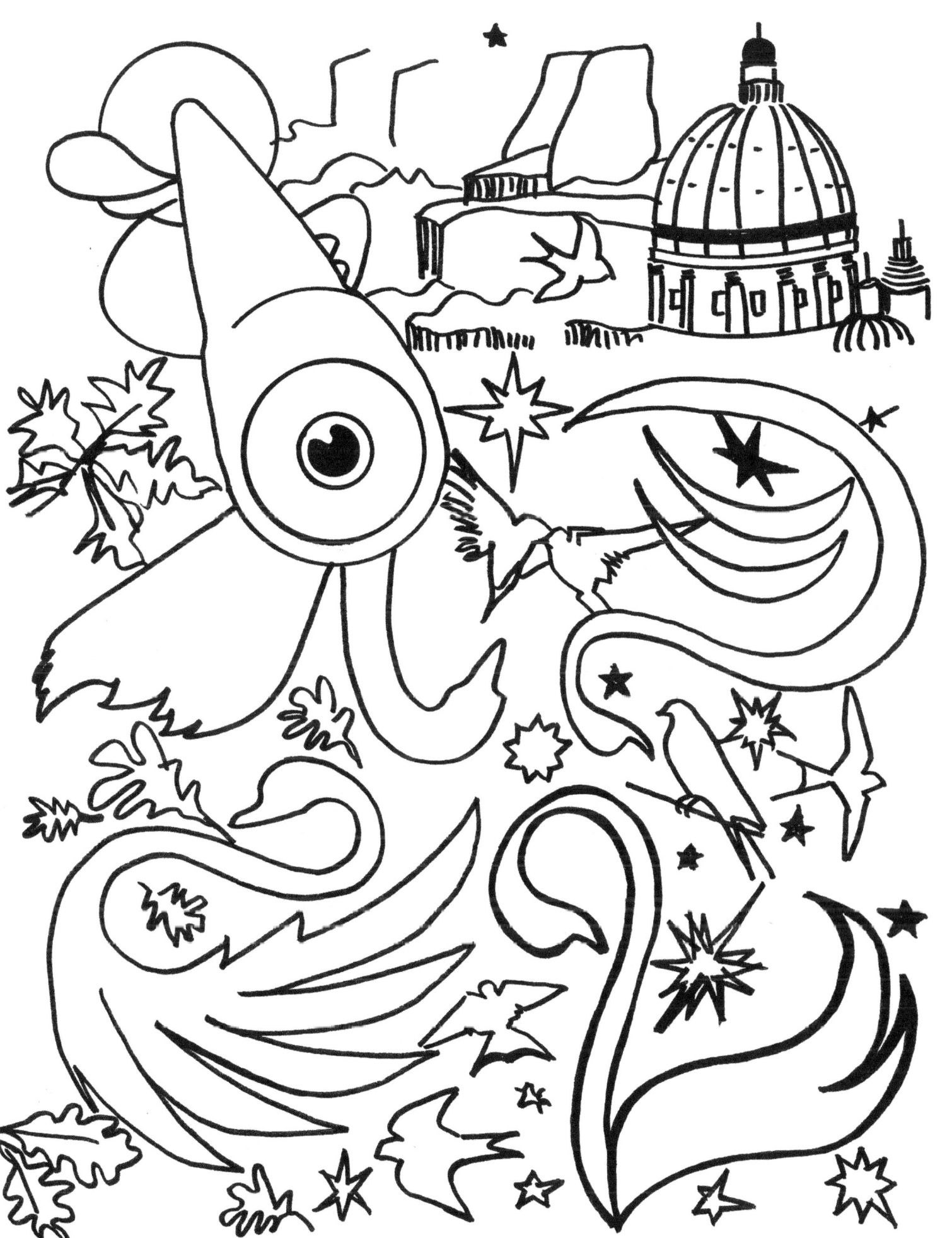

Laurinda Stockwell

Dianne Stromberg

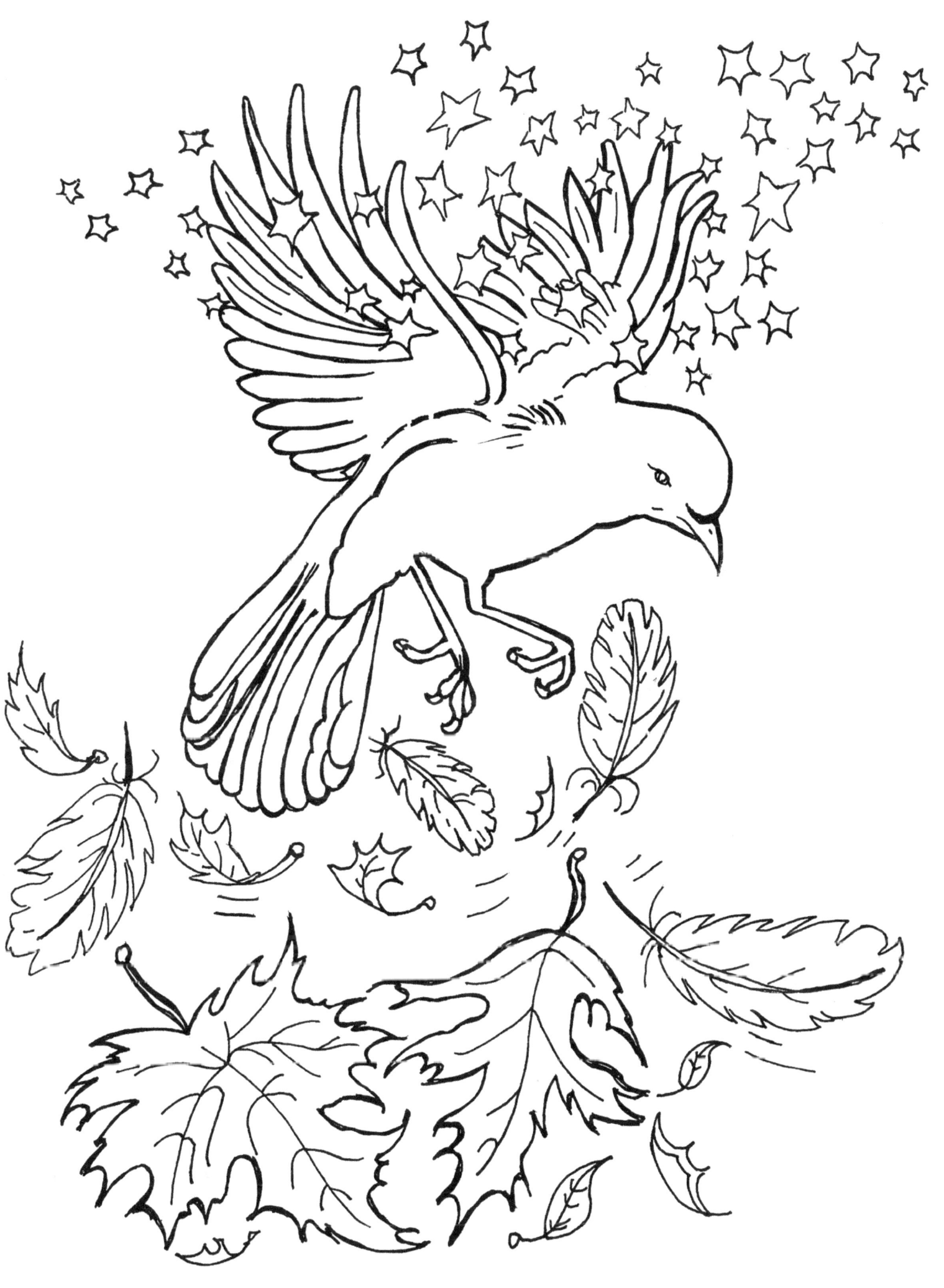

Anastasio Wrobel

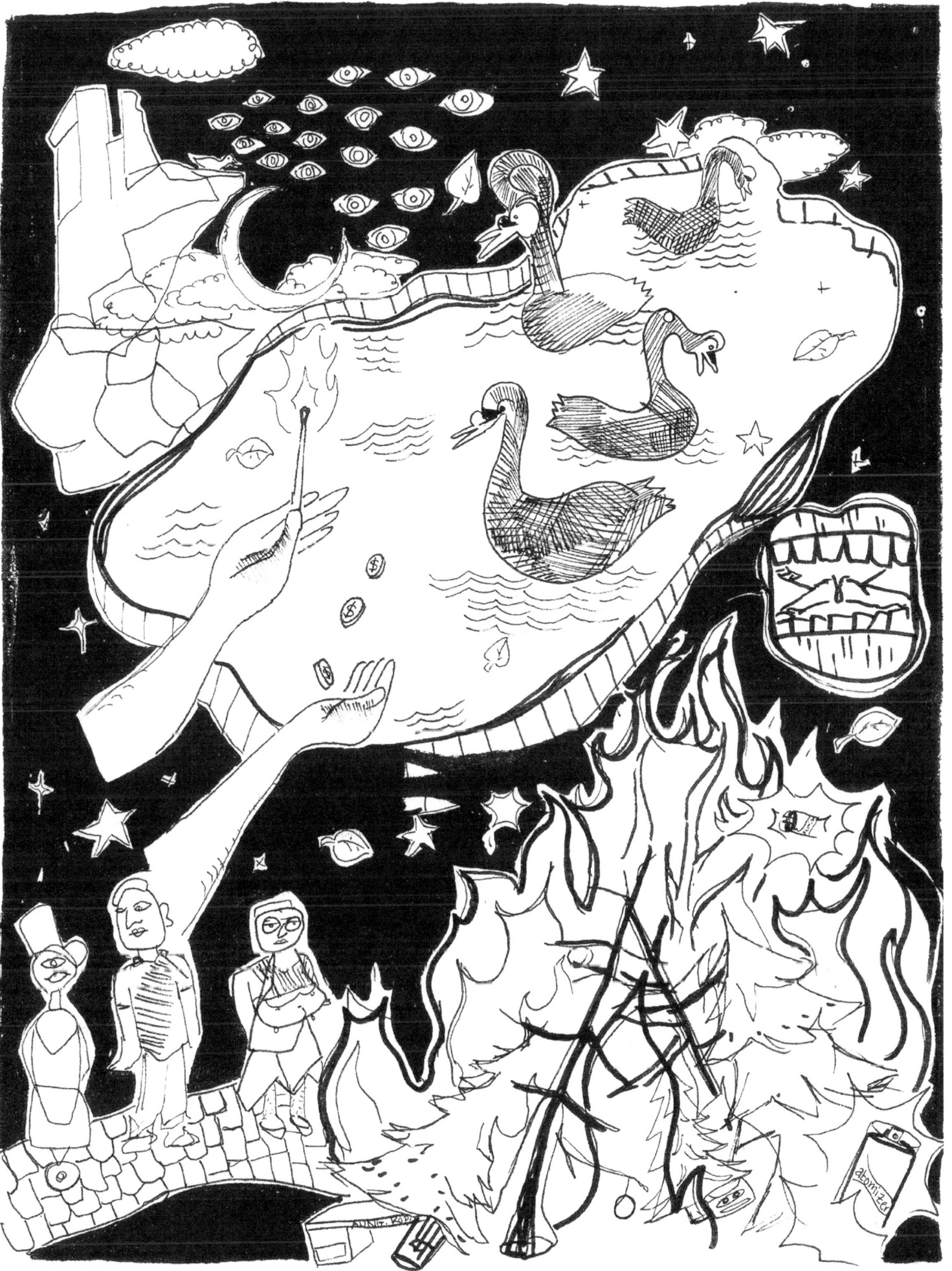

Joshua Atlas

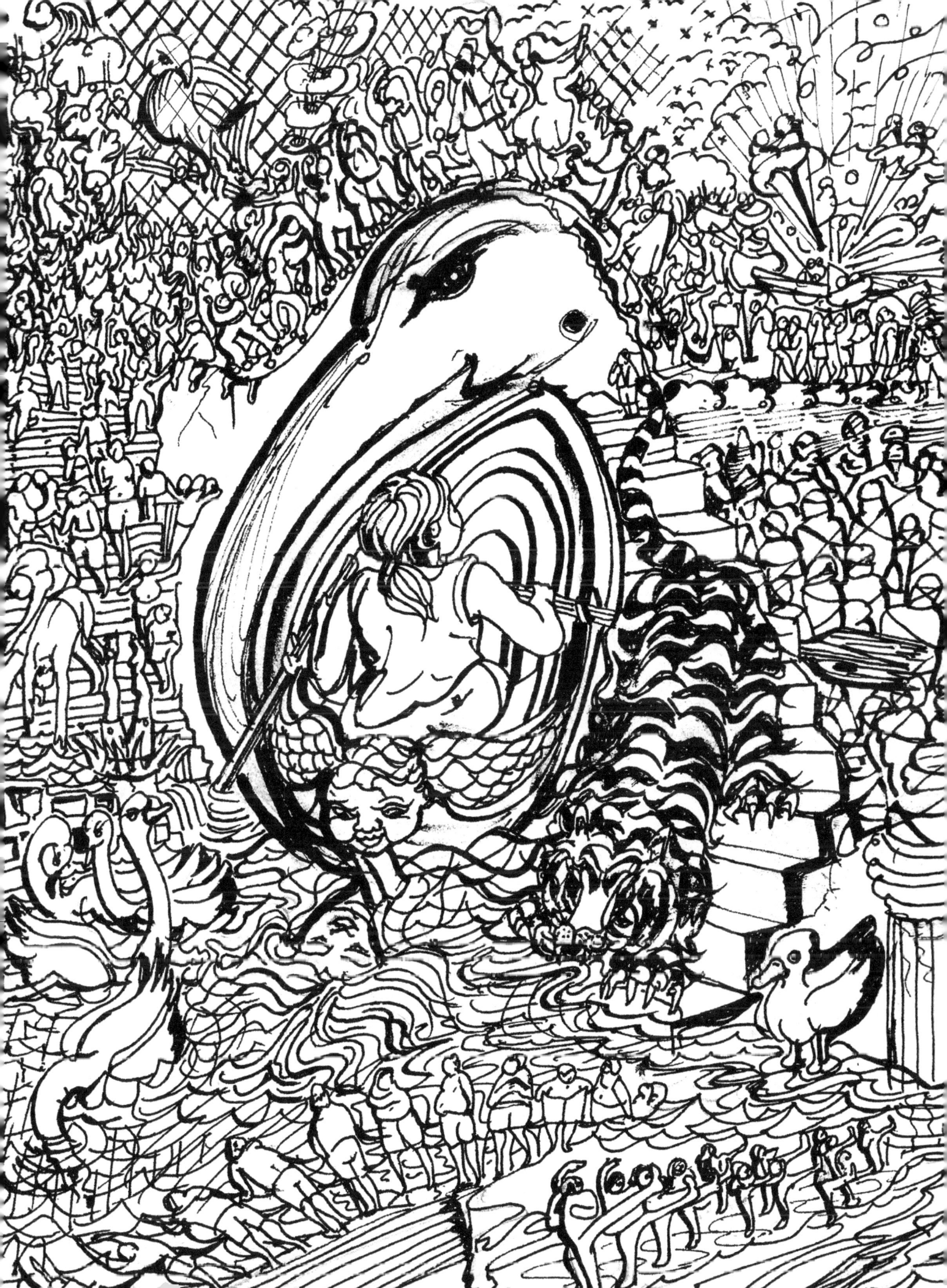

Sienna Heinemann

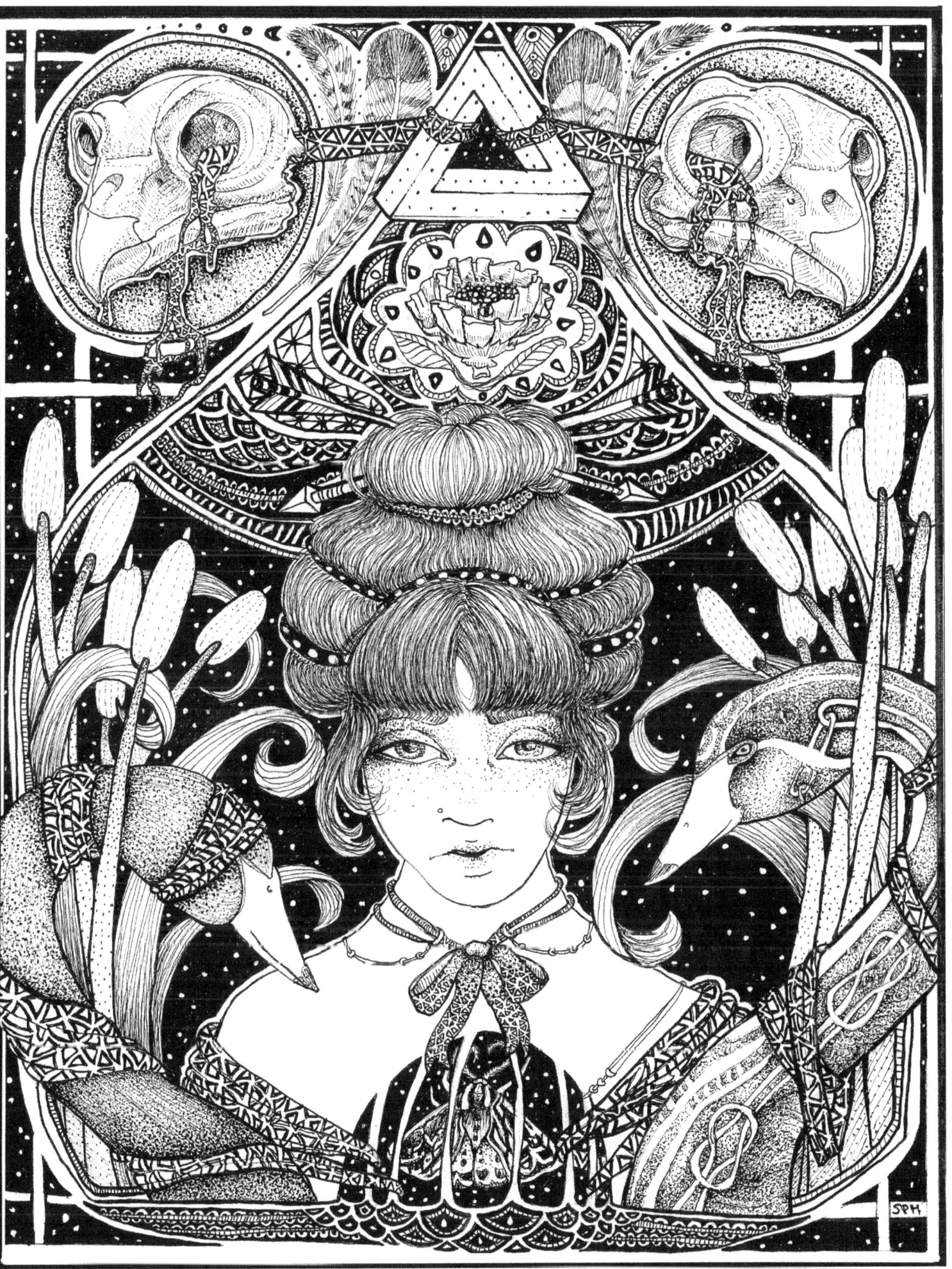

Alexandra Eldridge

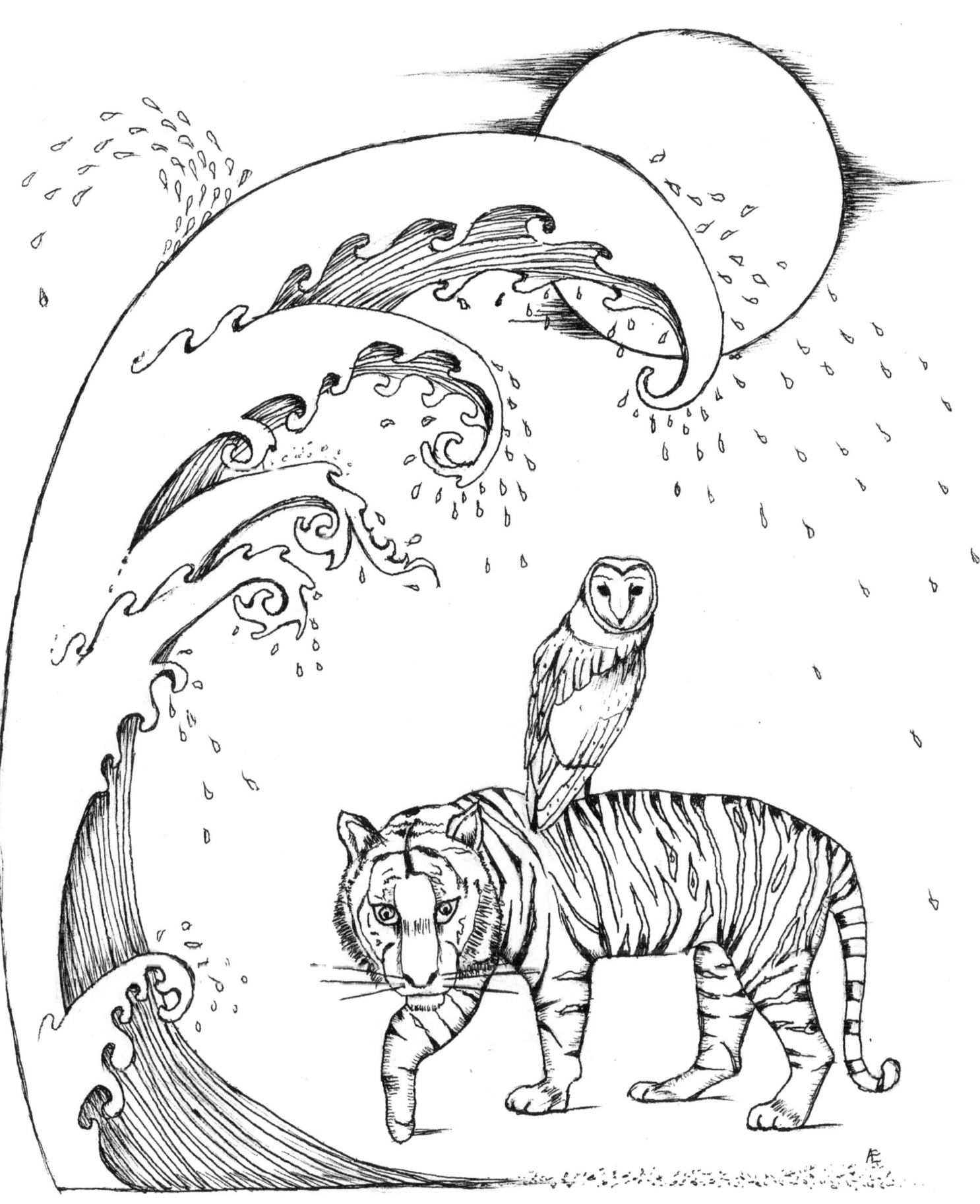

Joerael Julian Elliott

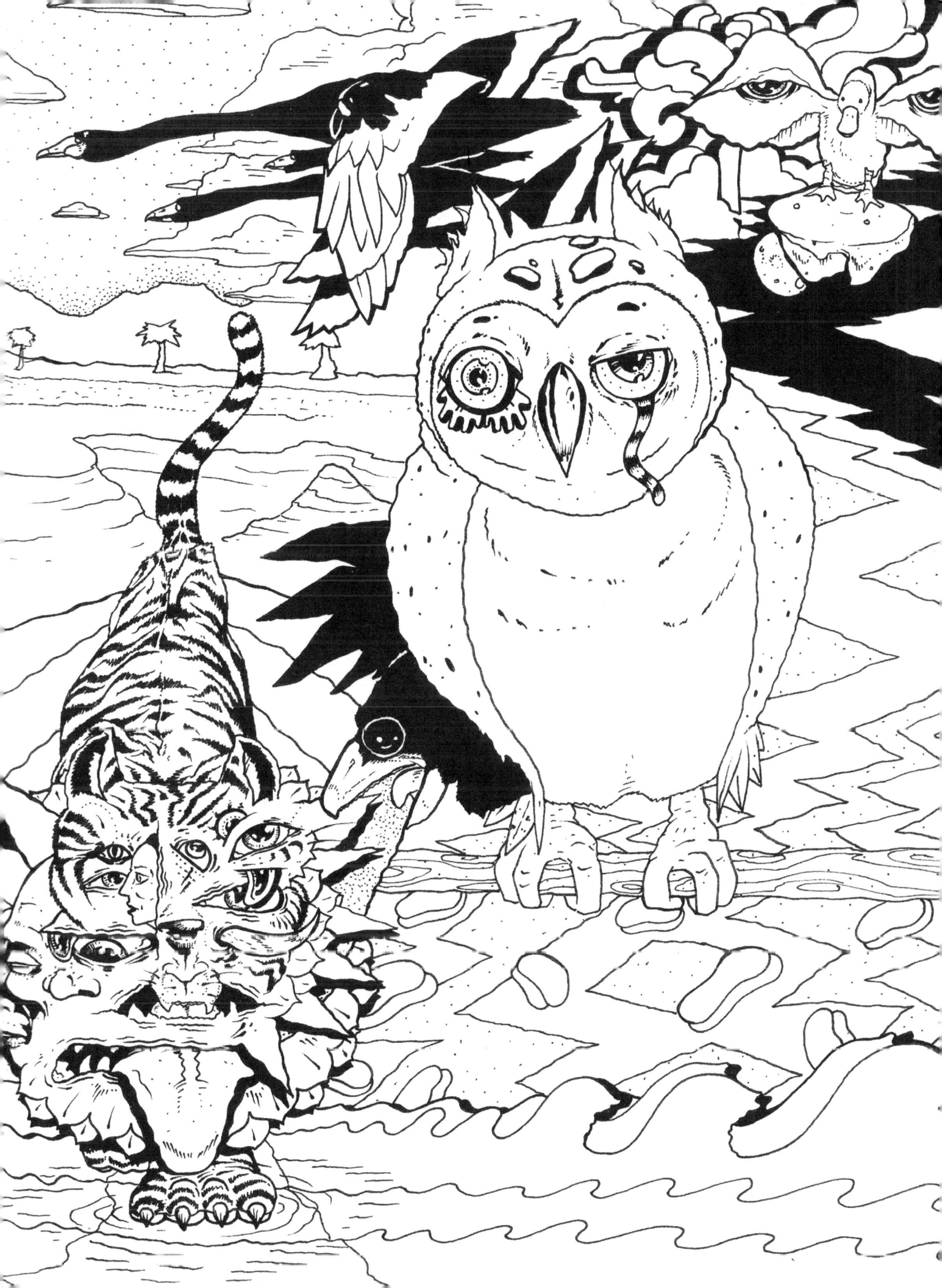

Katherine Lee

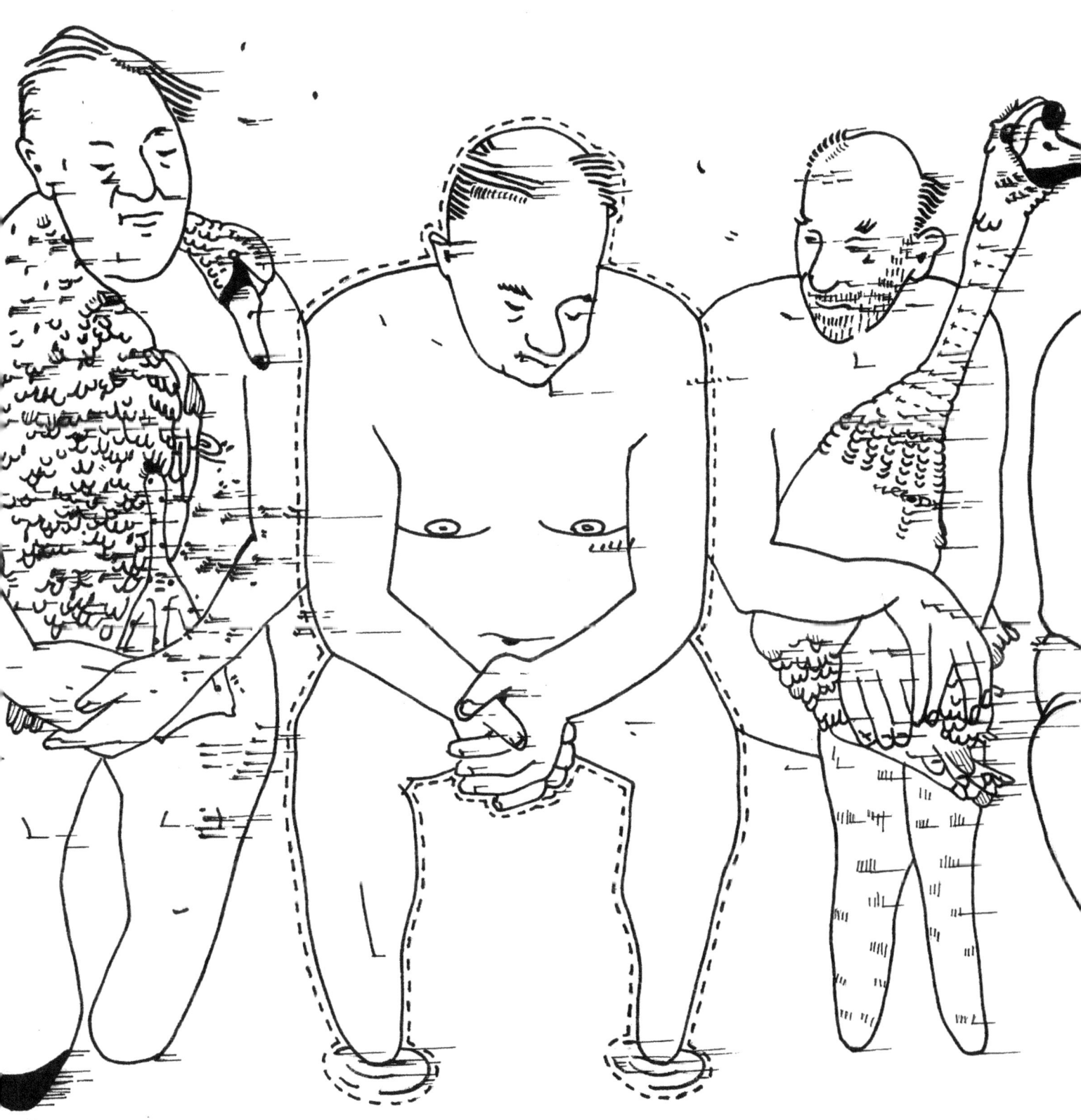

Jason Garcia

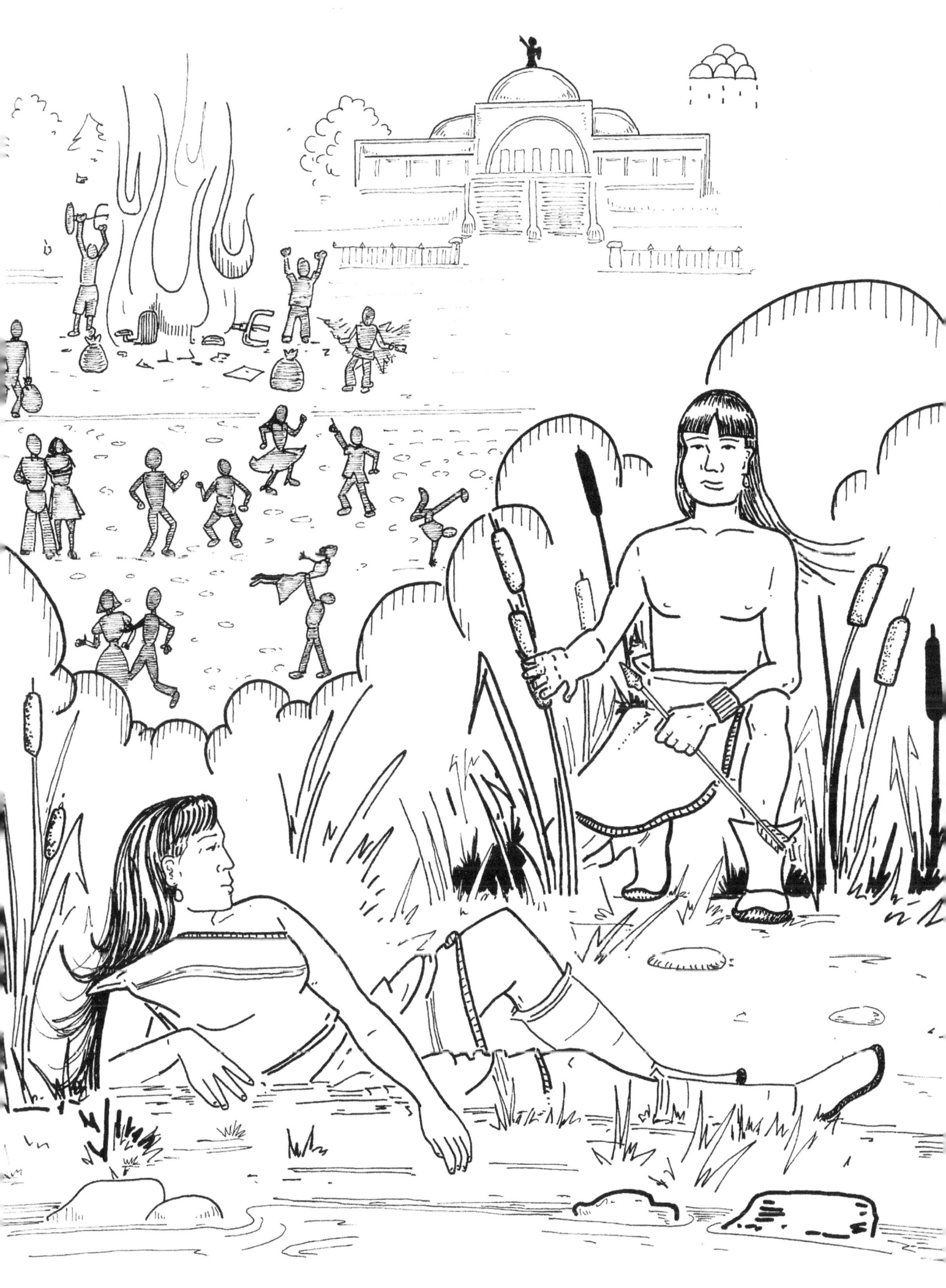

Betty Yozell

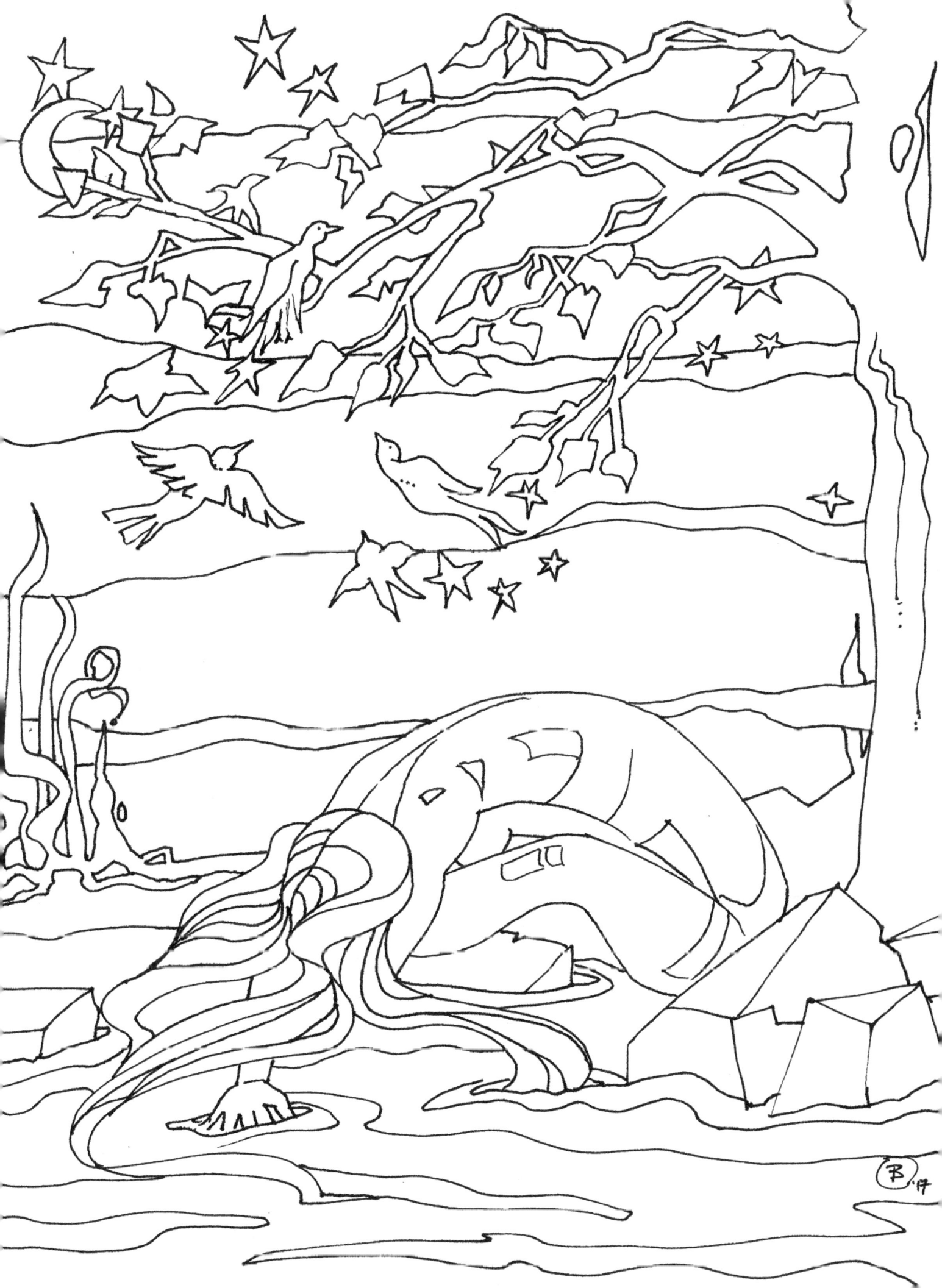

Linda Vi Vona

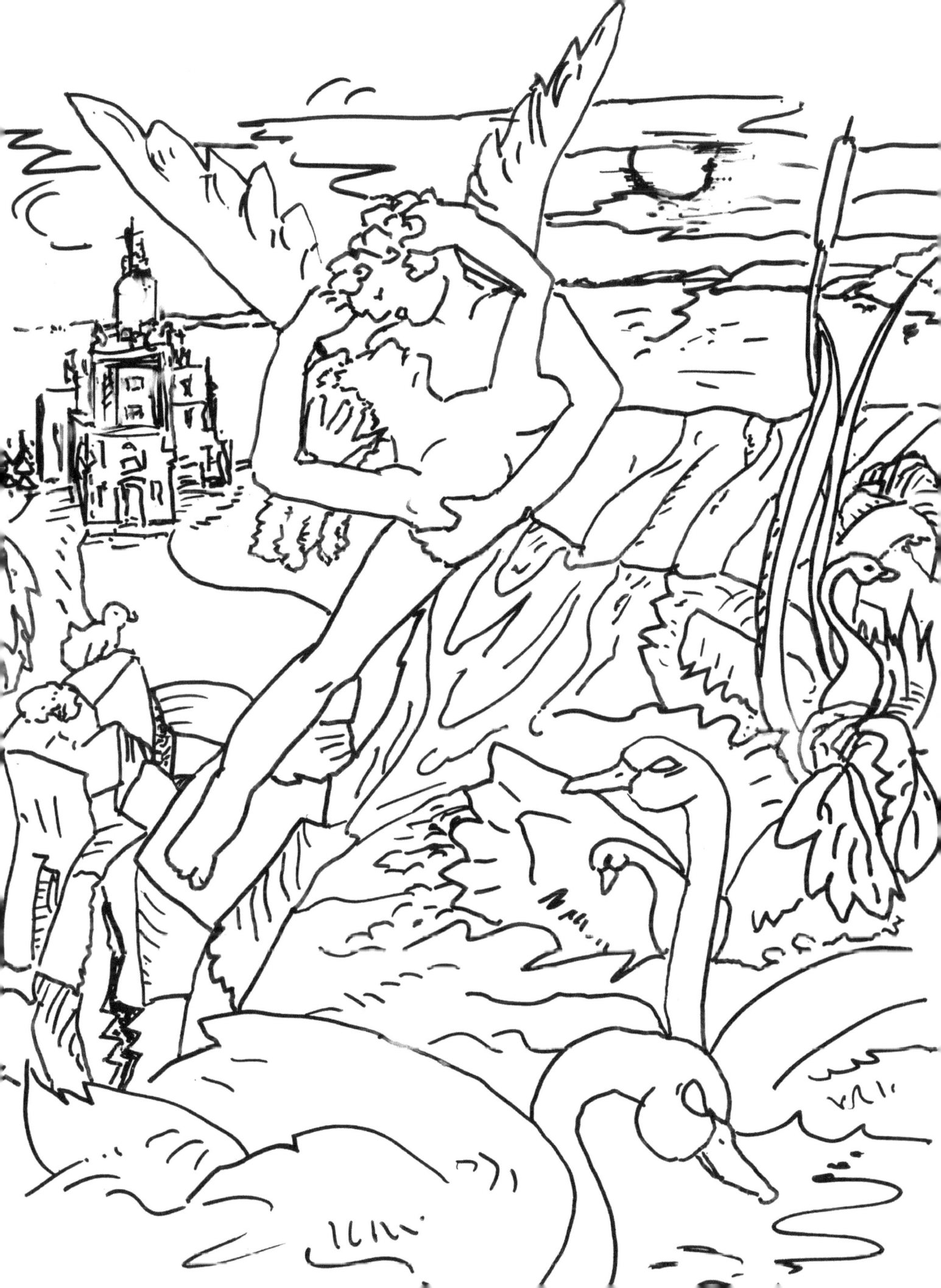

Daniel McCoy Jr.

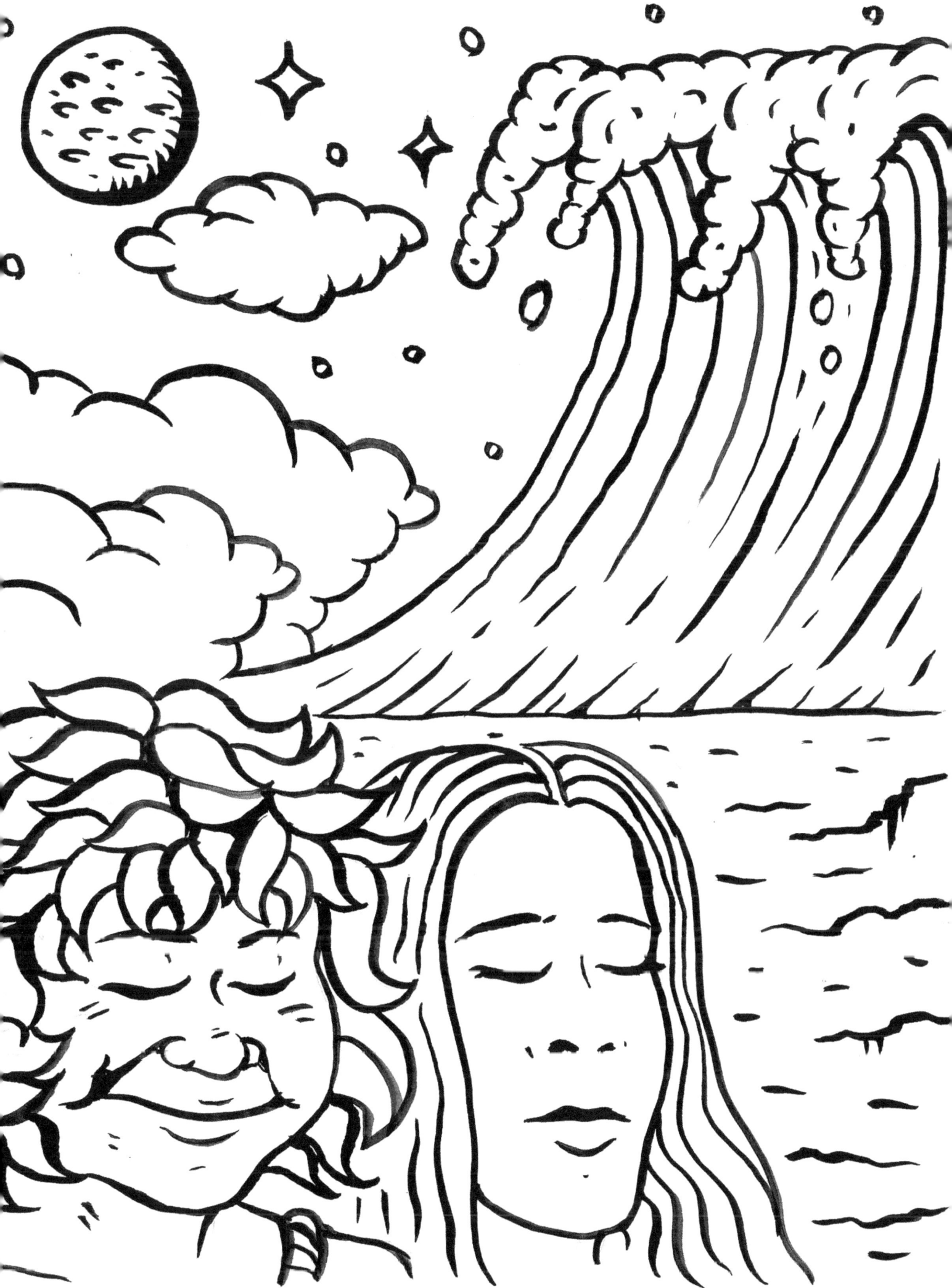

The Family of Talls

Jamie Figueroa

Once there was a family of talls—a father who was tall, a son who was tall, and a daughter who was tall. They lived in a tall house, on top of a hill, at the end of a dirt road surrounded by trees.

In the mornings, without fail, the tall father swept the clouds from the sky. Then, he woke his children by singing, "It's another beautiful day." The children unfolded their long legs while the father helped them search for their smiles. Sometimes their smiles were hidden in the hamper, or still hanging from their toothbrushes, or sometimes even stuck to the bottoms of their shoes. When the tall son and the tall daughter had found their smiles and fixed them to their faces, and when their legs were sturdy beneath them, they trotted alongside the river all the way to school.

While the children were at school, the tall father tended to the trees on the land surrounding his house. When he found a tree that was wider than it was tall, he bent over it, hands gripping the trunk, pulling on the tree, making it taller. The trees were grateful for the help, as it meant being that much closer to the sun, to the heart of the sky.

One day when the father was studying trees in need of being stretched, he came upon a shrub of a thing. He gripped the trunk, but when he pulled, it did not budge. Again, he tried but nothing. The tree was stubborn. No matter how many times he pulled, it did not grow. Soon, it was nearly dark. The father remembered his children. He had not been at home to greet them as he always did when they returned from school. Quickly, he strode down the hill, one very long leg, and then the other.

The tall son and the tall daughter jumped up and down at the sight of their tall father. He held them in his arms, but instead of his usual song and laughter, there were tears. "What's the matter?" his children wanted to know. They had never seen their father without his smile.

"Today," the father said, "was a sad day. I found a tree that did not want to be tall." The father began to cry. For the first time in his life, he felt very small. "There was nothing I could do," he told his children.

The tall son and the tall daughter were quite wise, and they surprised their tall father when they said, first the son and then the daughter, "Oh, Papa. Not everything wants to be tall. Not everything wants to be happy." This was confusing for the father, and made him feel not like a man at all. And even though he couldn't fully understand his children's words, he sensed the truth in them.

At that, the tall son and the tall daughter each took one of his hands, and led him outside where the stars glittered in the dark sky. All three were quiet as they waited for what they did not know. As they waited, they felt how long their legs were. They felt their feet upon the ground, and while they did not exactly feel happy, they felt something else, they felt strong. As they looked into the darkness, and watched the glittering of stars, their strength began to feel like magic. It twinkled inside them. Who knew what the next day would bring?

Crockett Bodelson

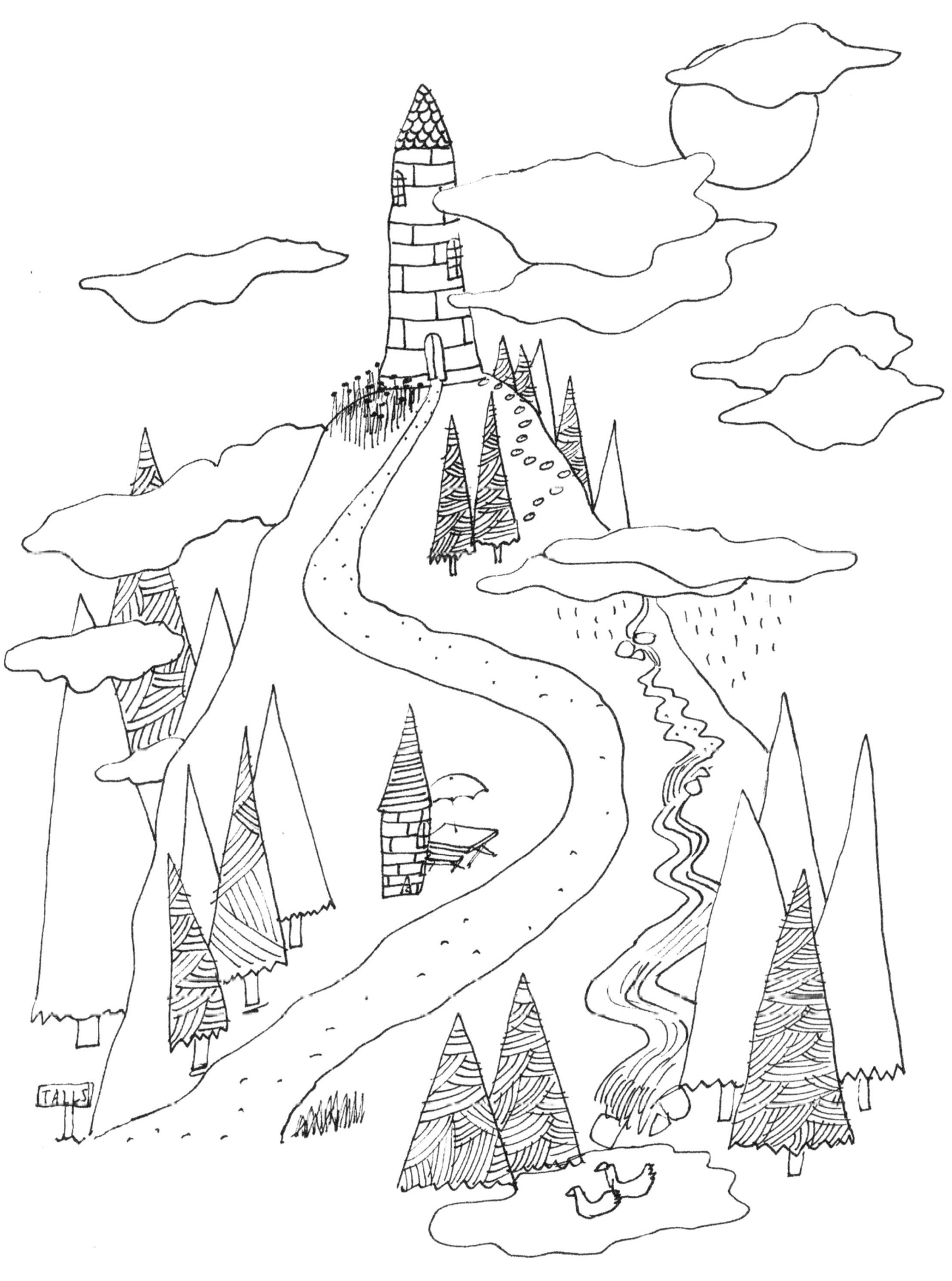

Lisa Flynn

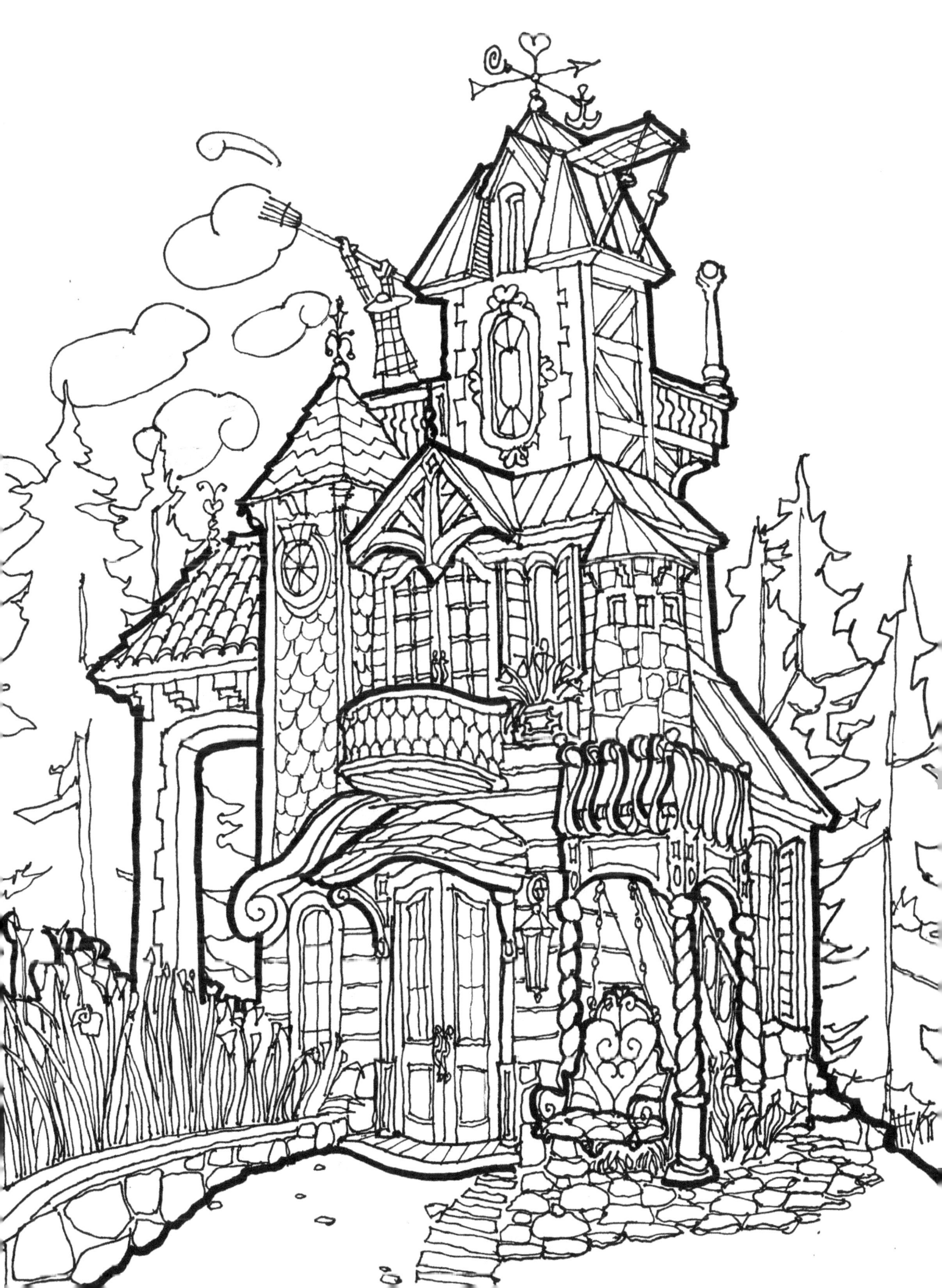

Eliza Naranjo Morse

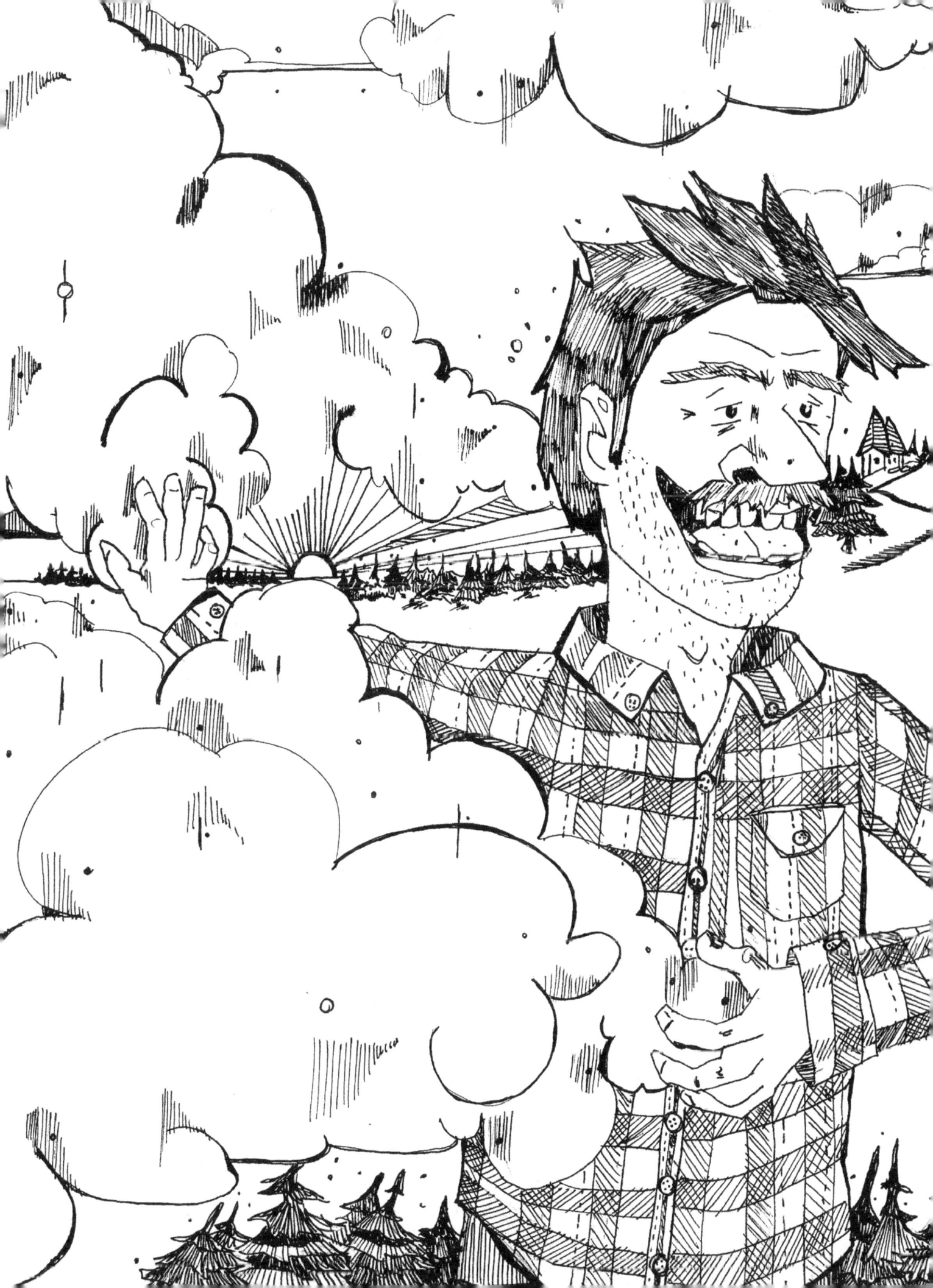

Arlene Ory

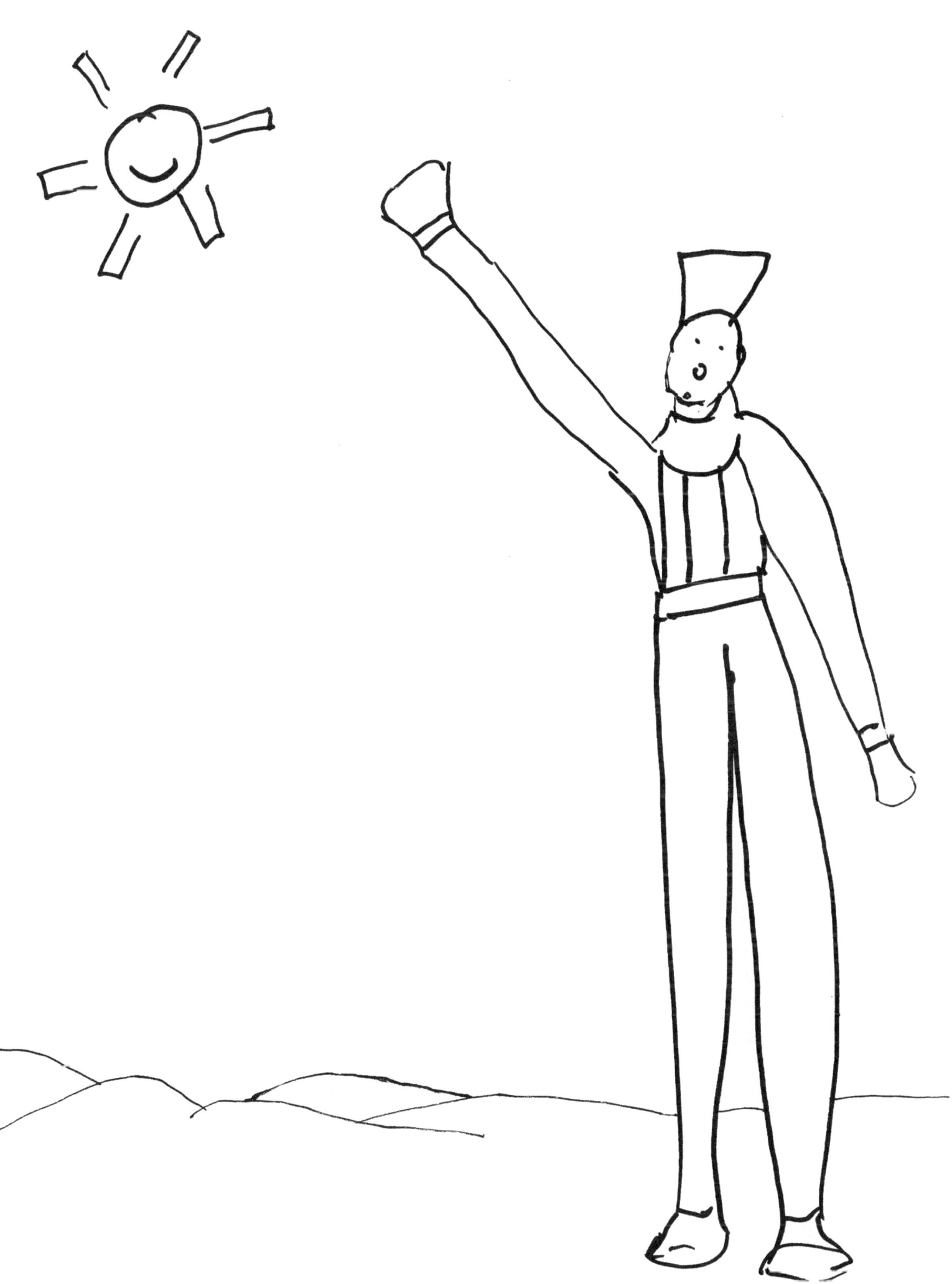

Israel Haros Lopez

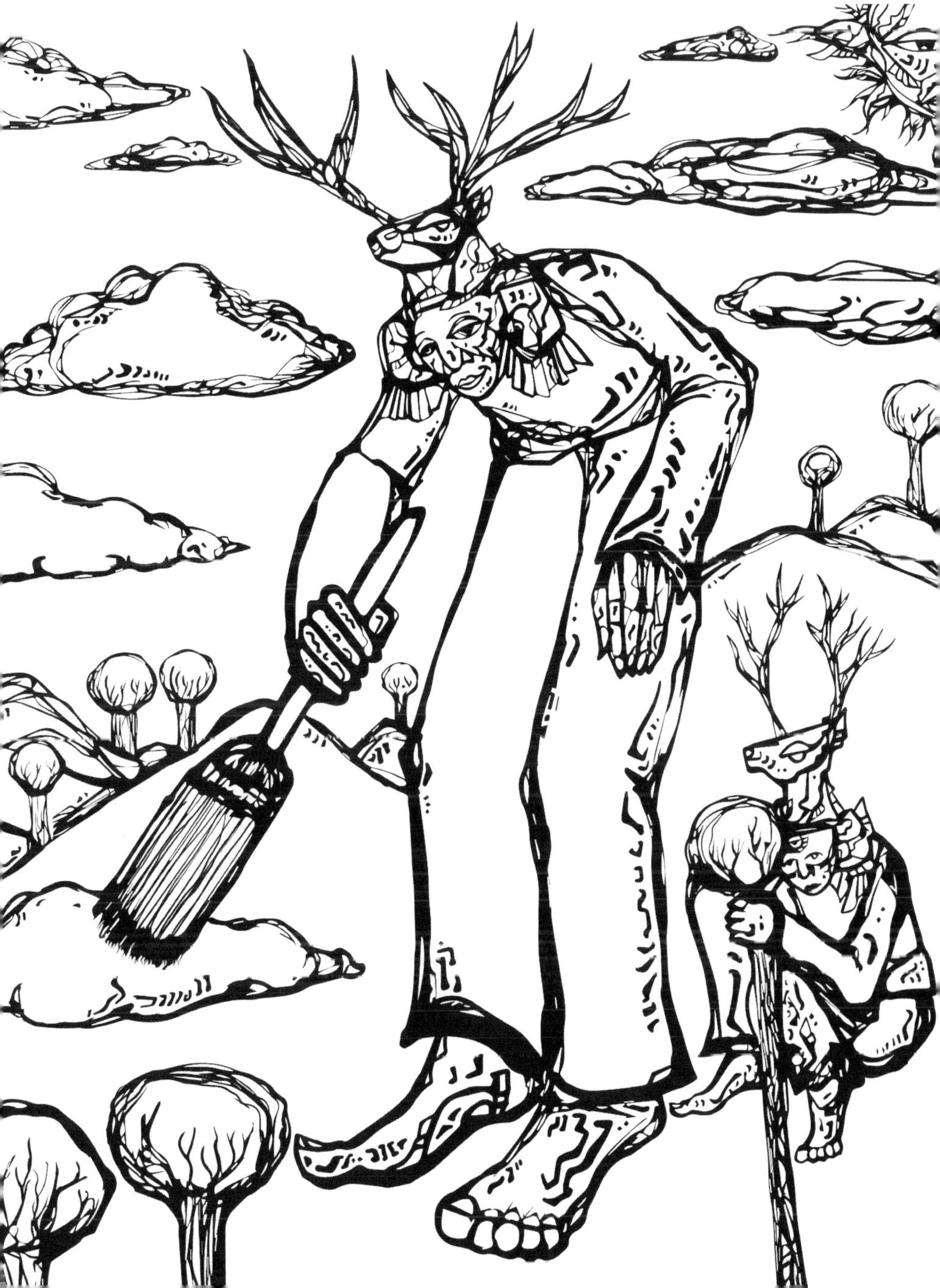

Rick Stevens

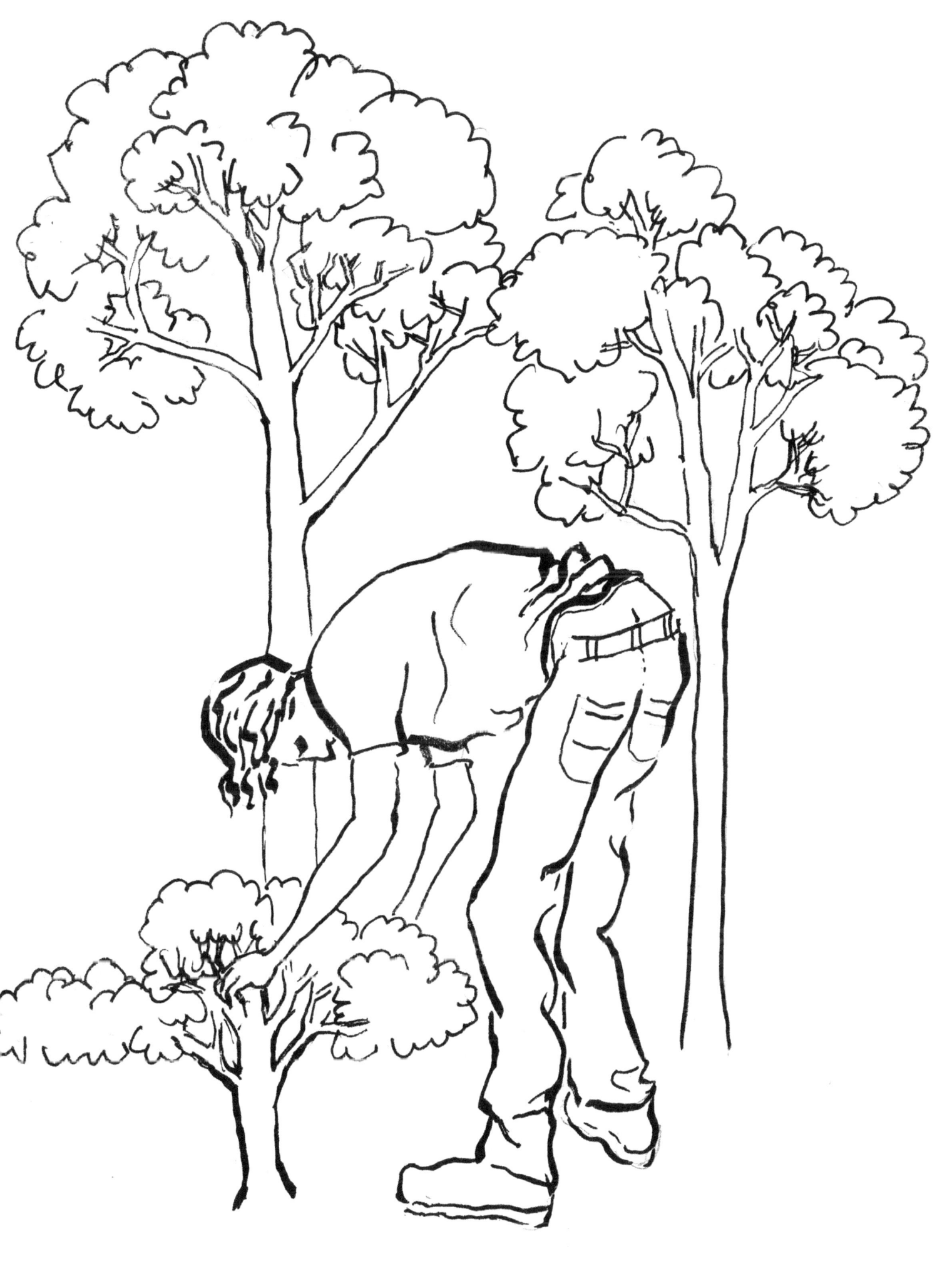

Holly Grimm

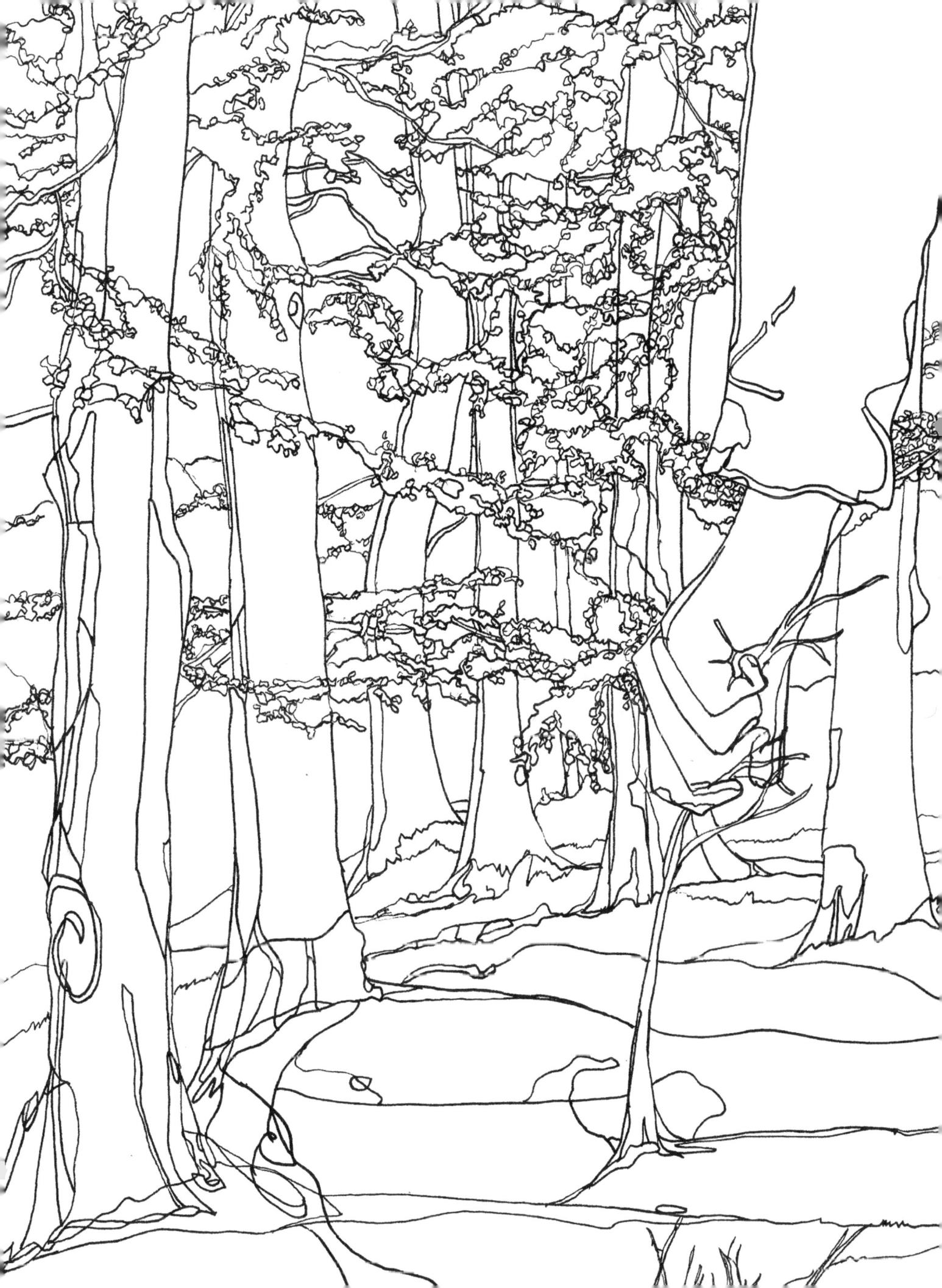

David Leigh

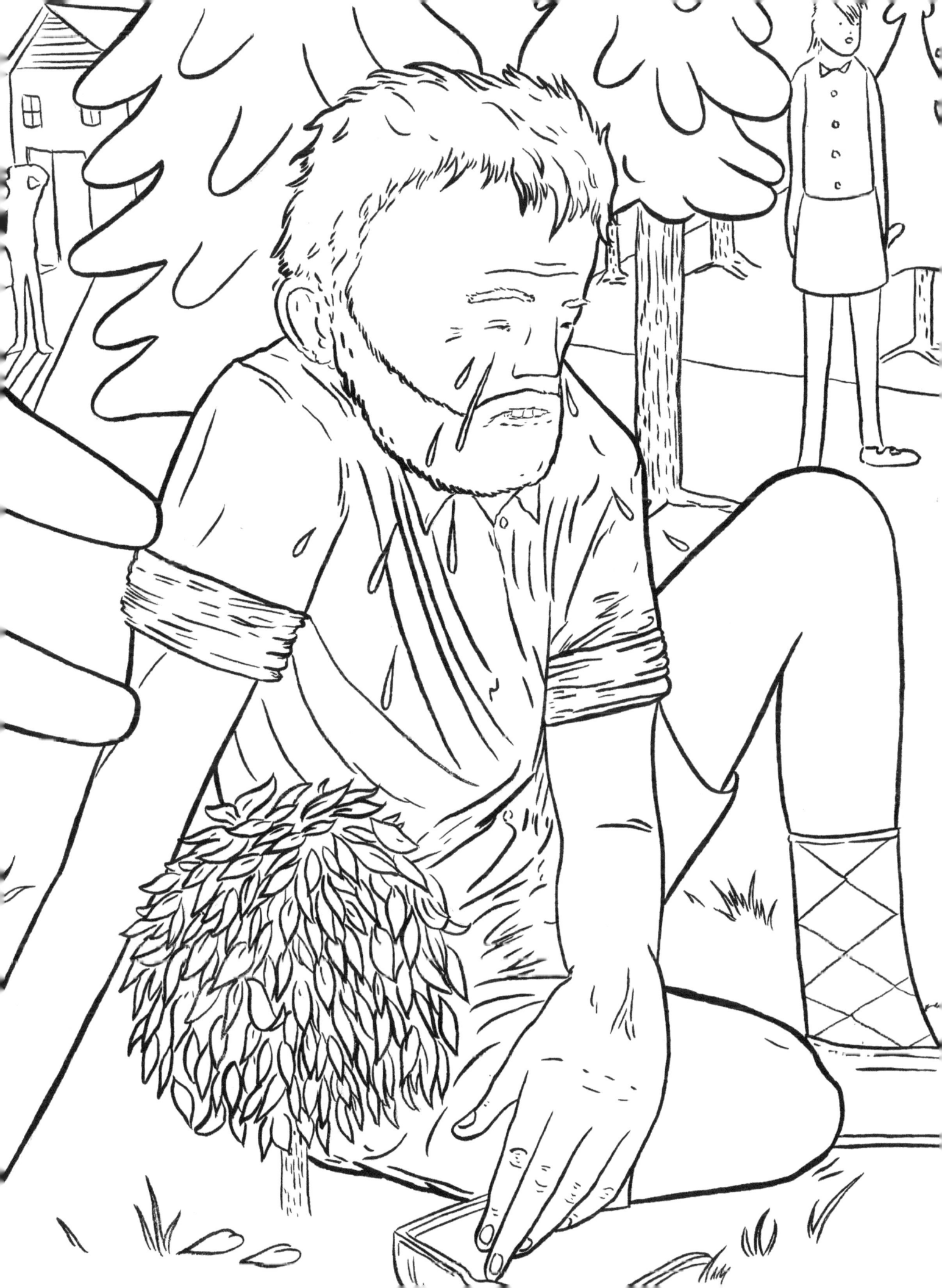

Rose Simpson

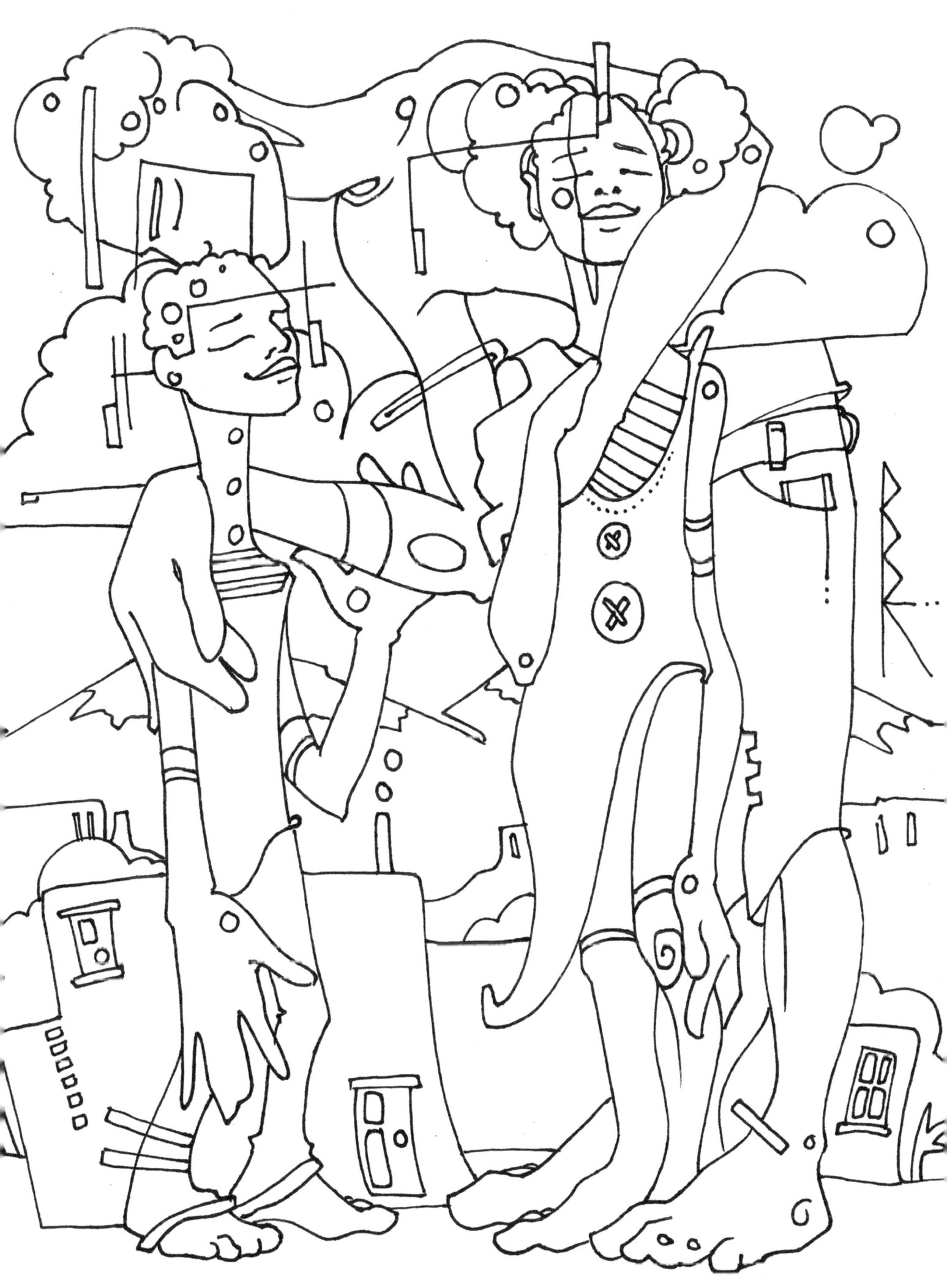

Tracy Cook Wein

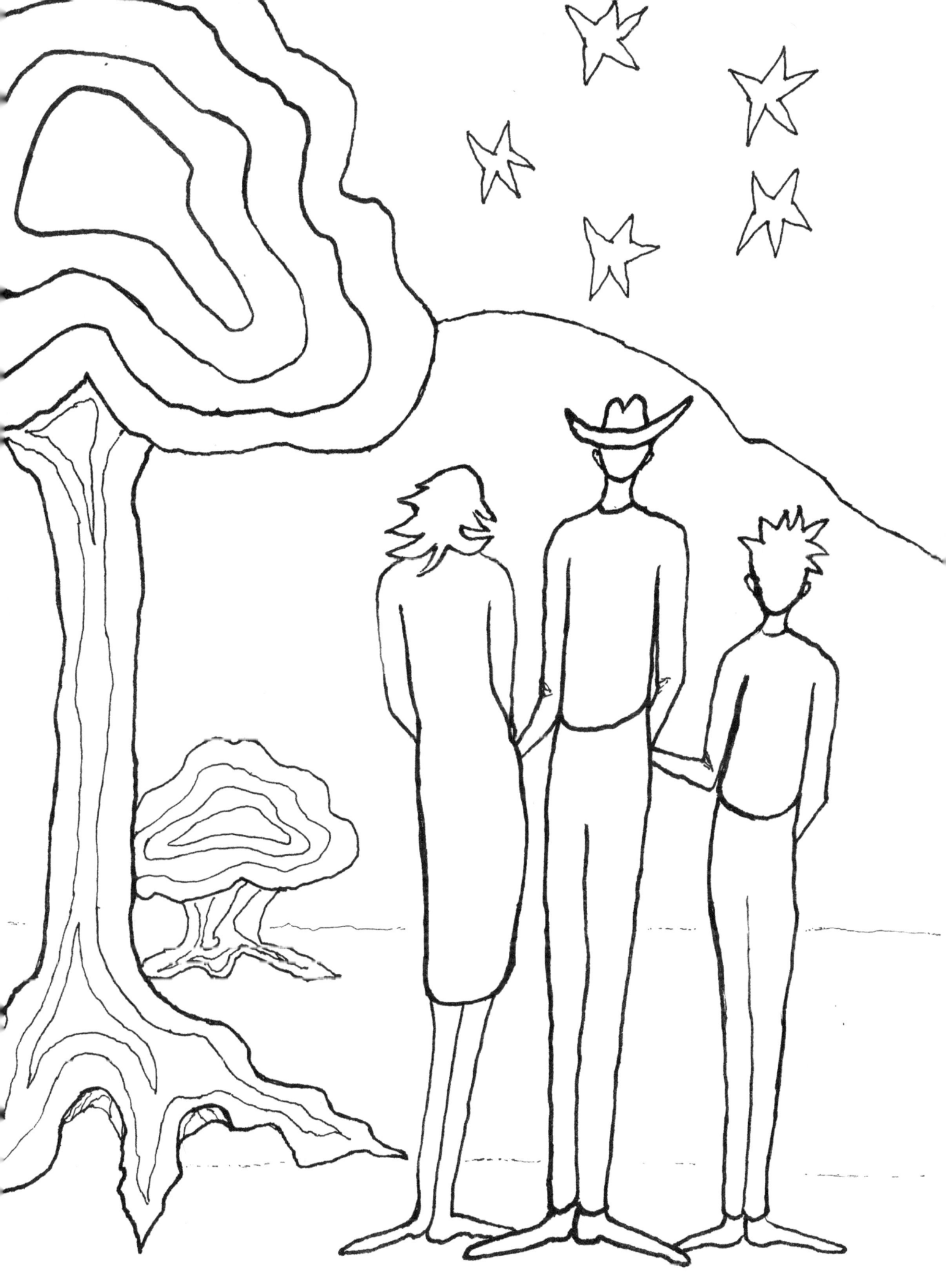

Jerry Wellman

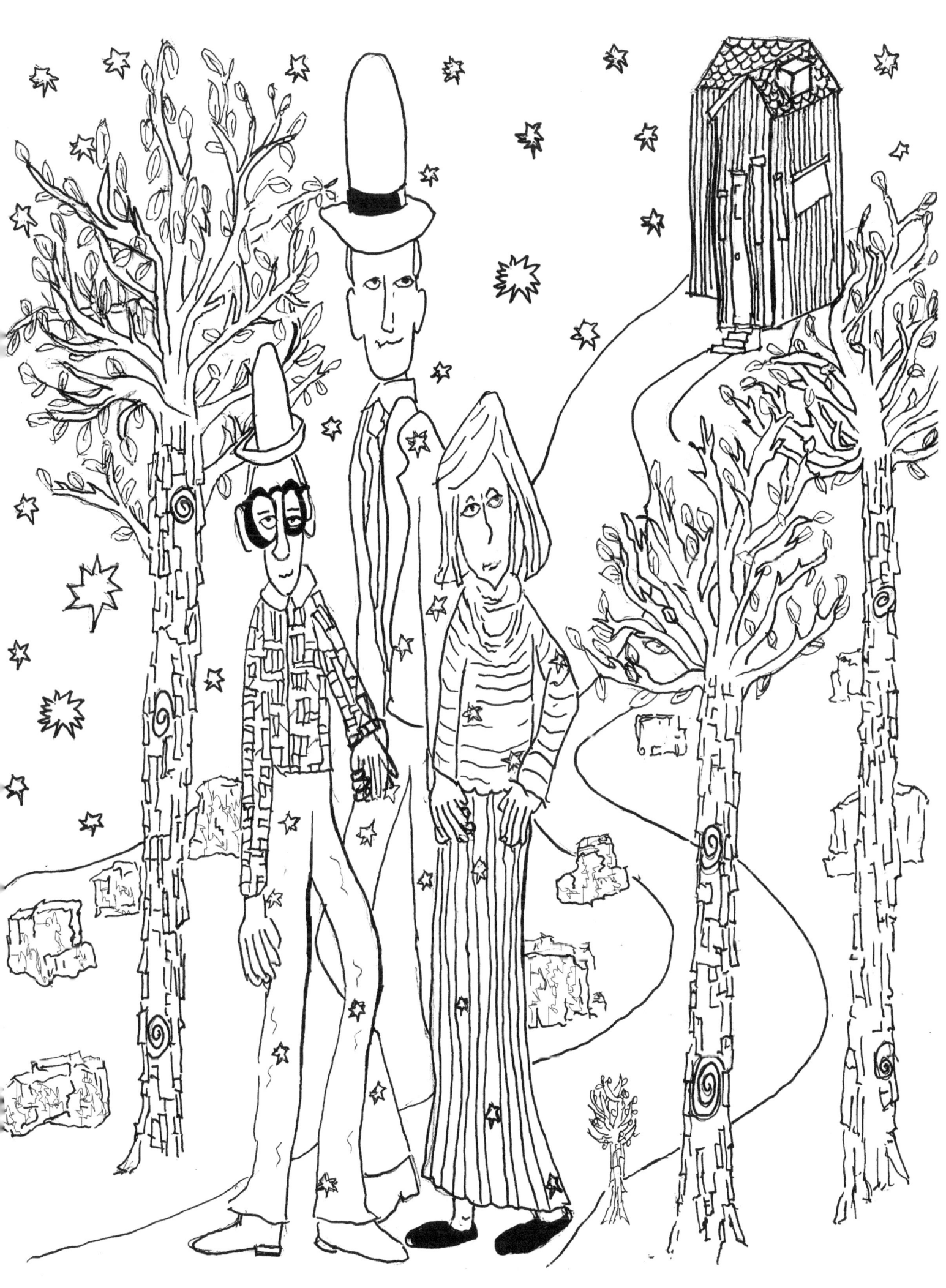

Erika Wanenmacher

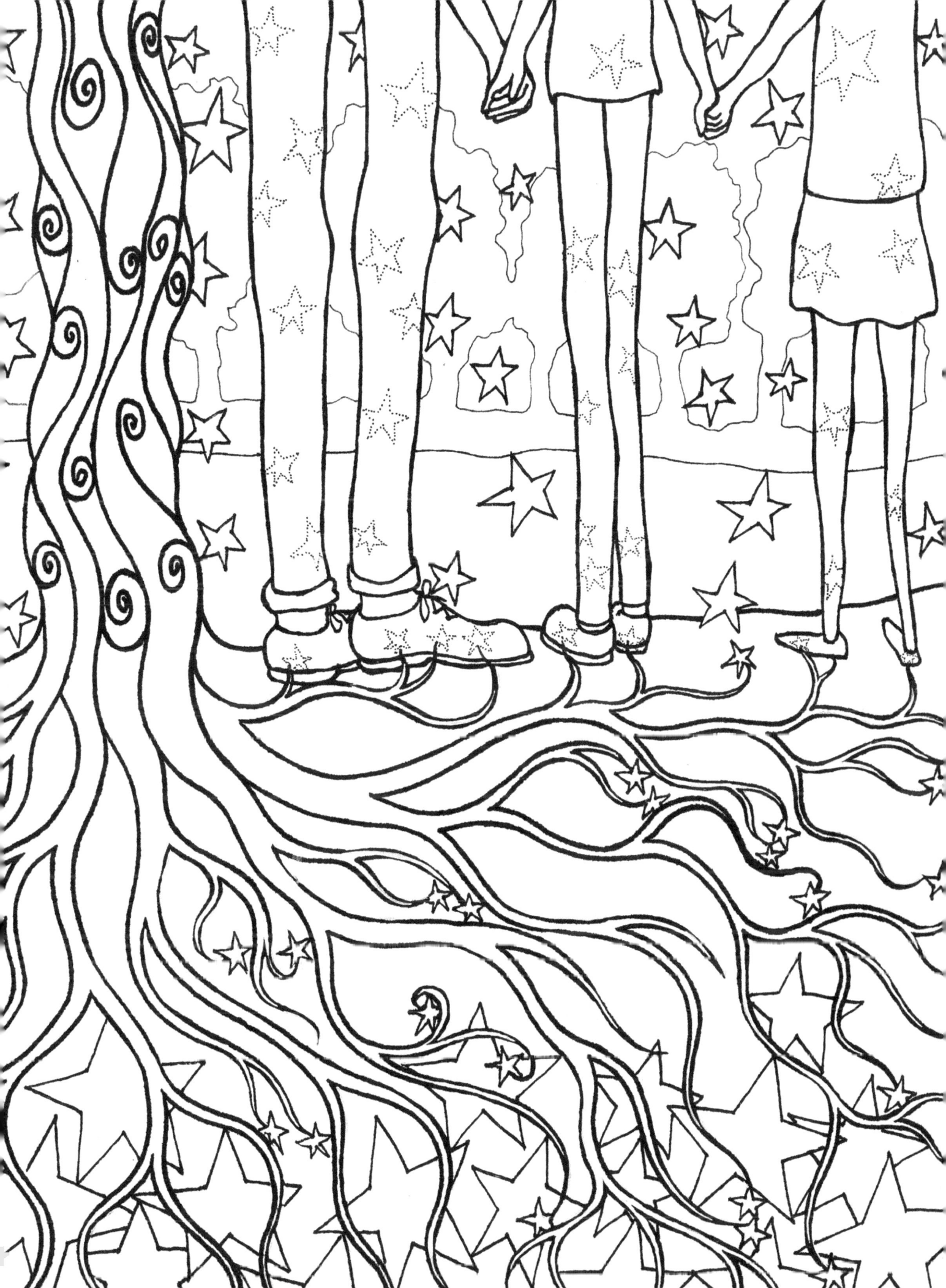

Claire Dunne

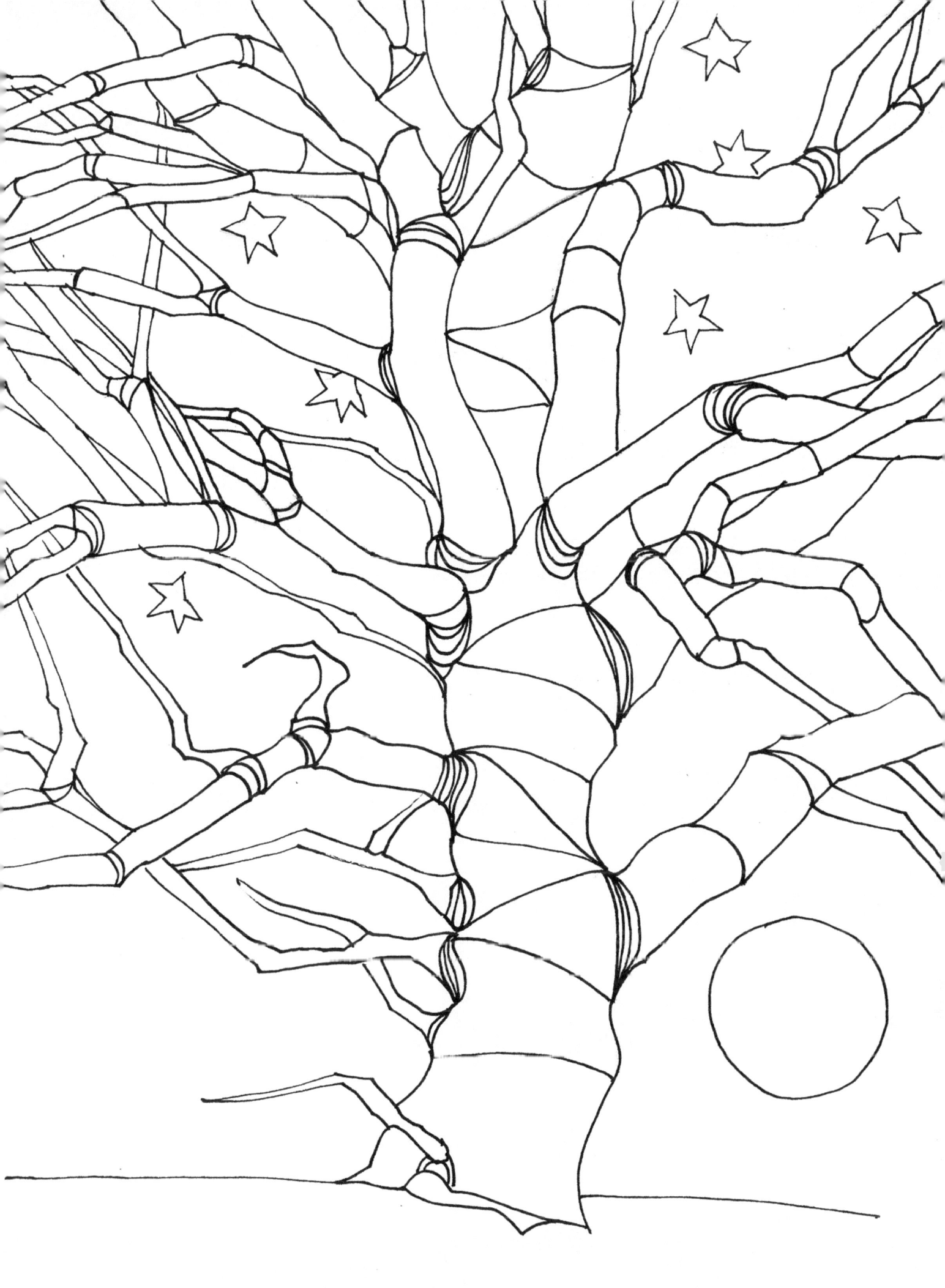

Johnny Blue

Nasario García

Johnny Blue (Juanito Azul) was an orphan who lived in a one-room shack near the village of Santa Clara. He had sparkling blue eyes, deemed an oddity among the local villagers, hence his nickname Johnny Blue. But he was also short, had long hands and one leg was shorter than the other.

Because of his physical characteristics, whenever there was a fiesta in Santa Clara the mothers did not allow their daughters to dance with him. He was even shunned on St. John's Day, June 24th, a popular day that honored persons bearing the name of Juan or Juana.

But an equally important festive day was St. Anne's Day, July 26th. Only women participated in the day's activities. Ladies of all ages wore colorful blouses and long pleated-skirts (pants were taboo) and rode their beautiful horses side-saddle to celebrate the occasion. Young girls used regular saddles and engaged in horse races.

The day's celebration always culminated in a joyful evening dance, but, unlike in previous dances, a dramatic and unsuspected thing happened one night after the musicians, a violinist and a guitarist, returned from taking a break. Just as they picked up their instruments to resume playing, Johnny Blue walked into the dance hall. He was all dressed in blue: a blue shirt, blue trousers, blue kerchief, blue cowboy hat, and shiny blue boots. He approached the violinist, asked him for his violin, and started playing a beautiful waltz. The women were in awe.

"Wow! Who would have guessed that the young man with long hands could make such lovely music?" a surprised lady asked rhetorically.

The words scarcely escaped her mouth when a tall attractive young lady dressed in white entered the dance hall, strolled halfway across the floor, and paused. The music stopped. Dead silence ensued, whereupon Johnny Blue limped slowly toward her. "May I have this dance?" he asked courteously and he removed his hat.

"A waltz, if you will," he said to the musicians, and Johnny Blue and his partner glided back and forth across the floor with incredible ease and elegance amid ohs and ahs from the older women. The dance ended, he thanked the lady, and she left the dance floor.

"Ladies and gentlemen!" interrupted the guitarist. "The next number will be ladies' choice." Unexpectedly, and much to Johnny Blue's astonishment, all the girls lined up to dance with him, but he rejected each one.

Johnny Blue put on his hat, departed in a swagger, mounted Moro, his bluish-white horse and headed home. Along the way an owl hooted and kept appearing from fence post to fence post. "Could this be a bad omen?" Johnny Blue wondered silently since owls were said to possess supernatural powers. Suddenly, standing in the middle of the dirt road was a tall figure with glittering blue eyes. "Though I appeared at tonight's dance uninvited," remarked the feminine voice, "it was to show those mothers what an elegant dancer you are," at which point she vanished in the dark.

Johnny Blue then leaned forward and whispered to Moro, "Blue is not only the color of the heavens and symbolic of the human spirit but magical as well."

Matthew Mullins

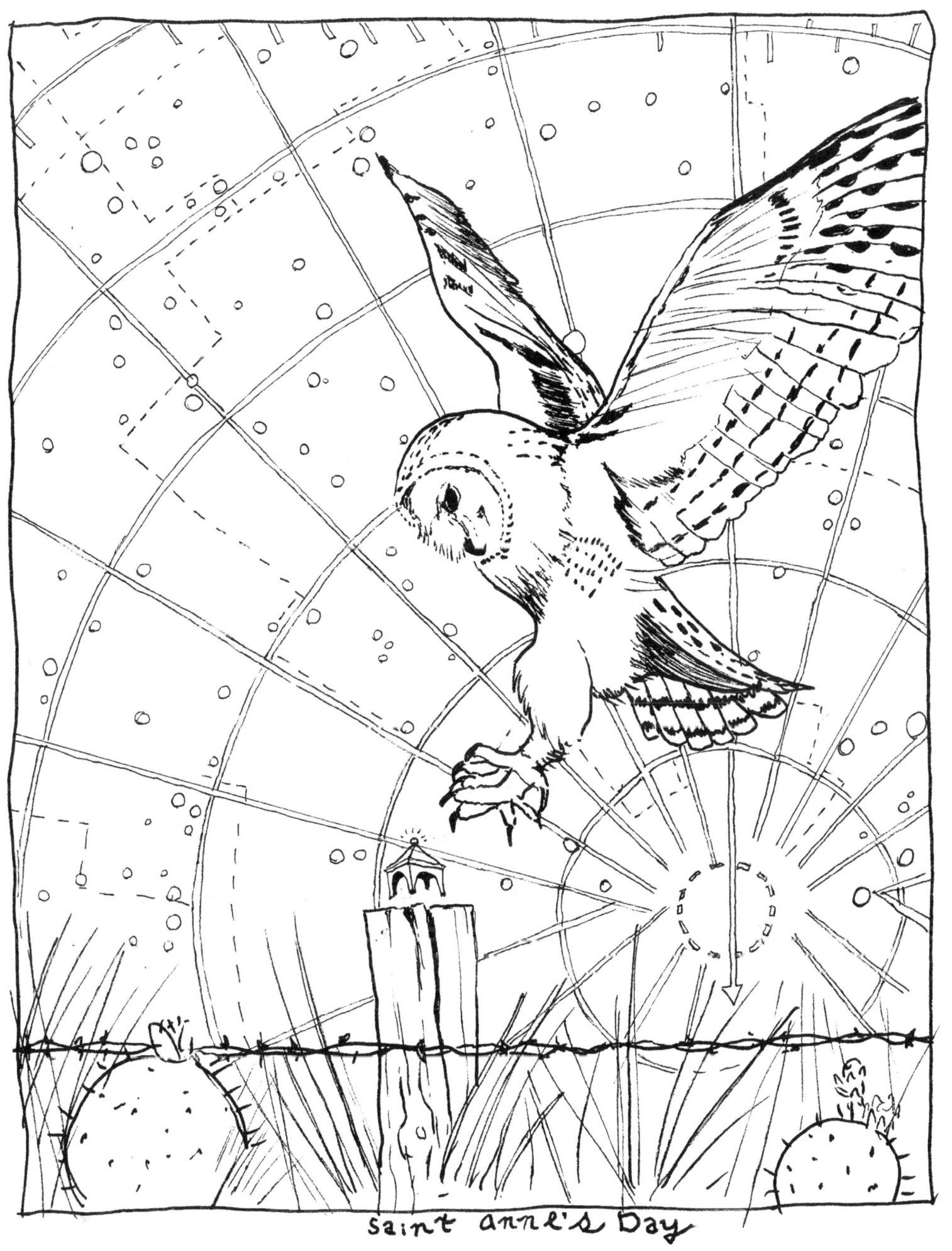

Saint anne's Day

Gwen Wells

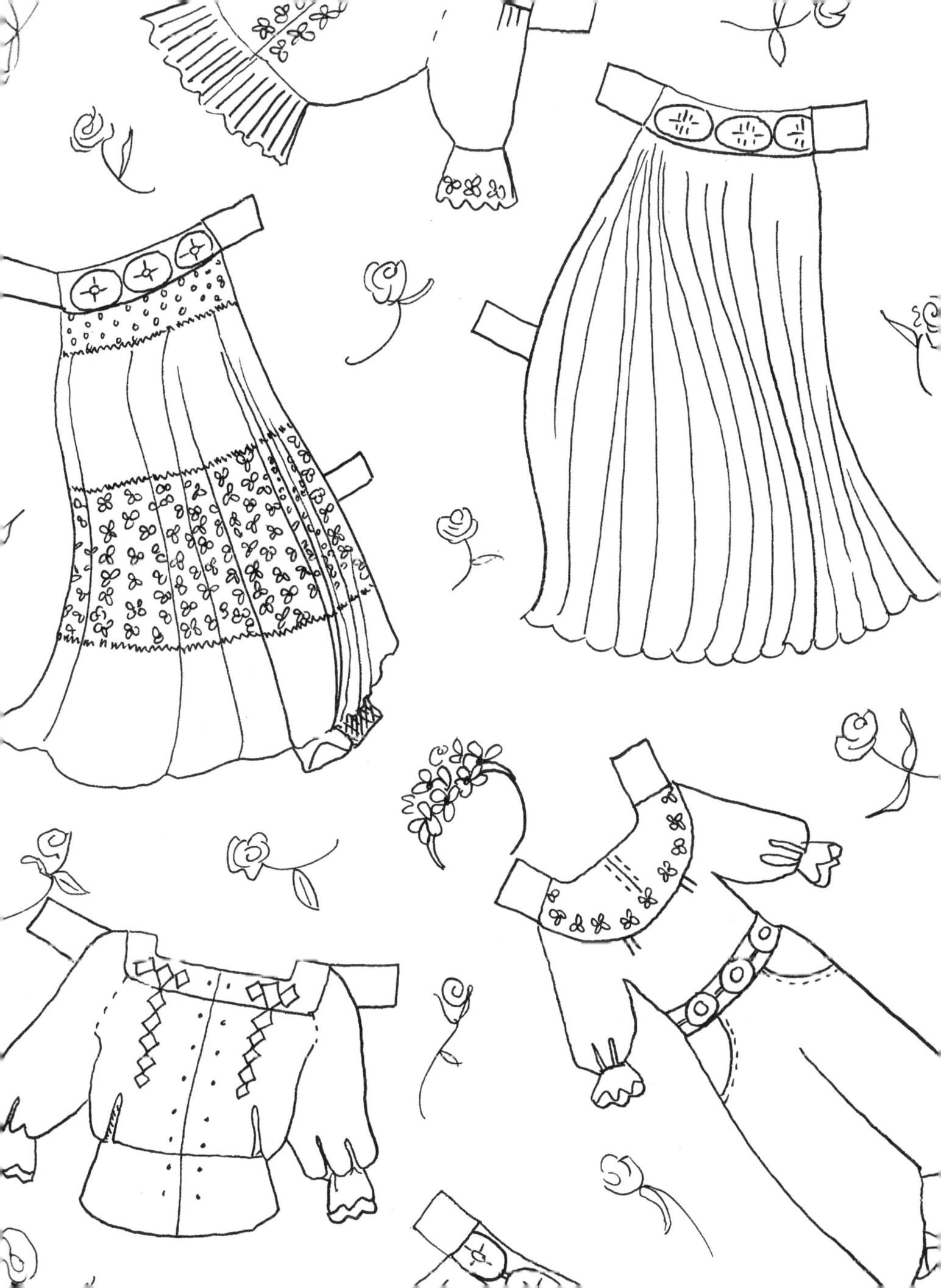

Kathleen McCloud

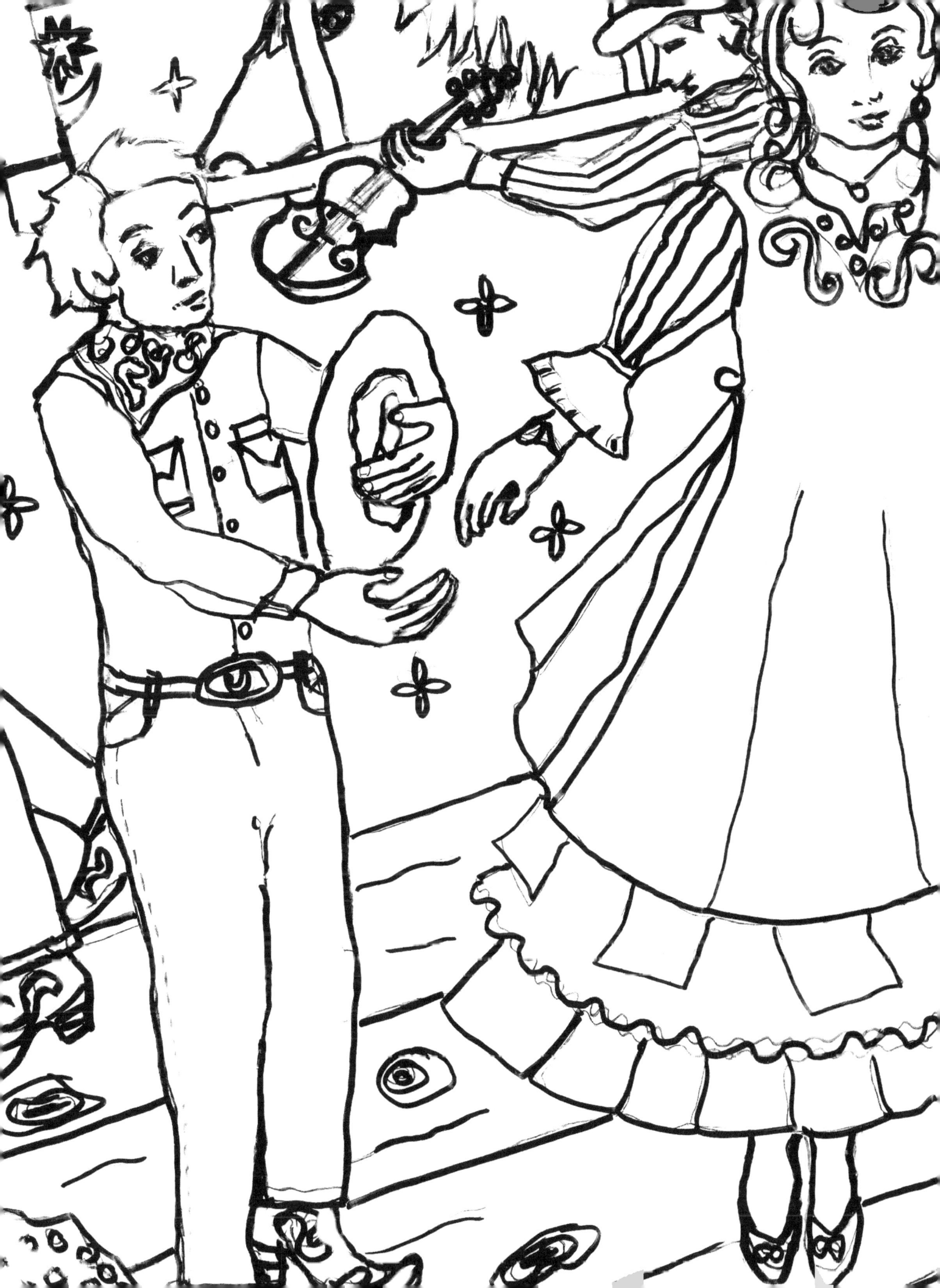

Rita Bard

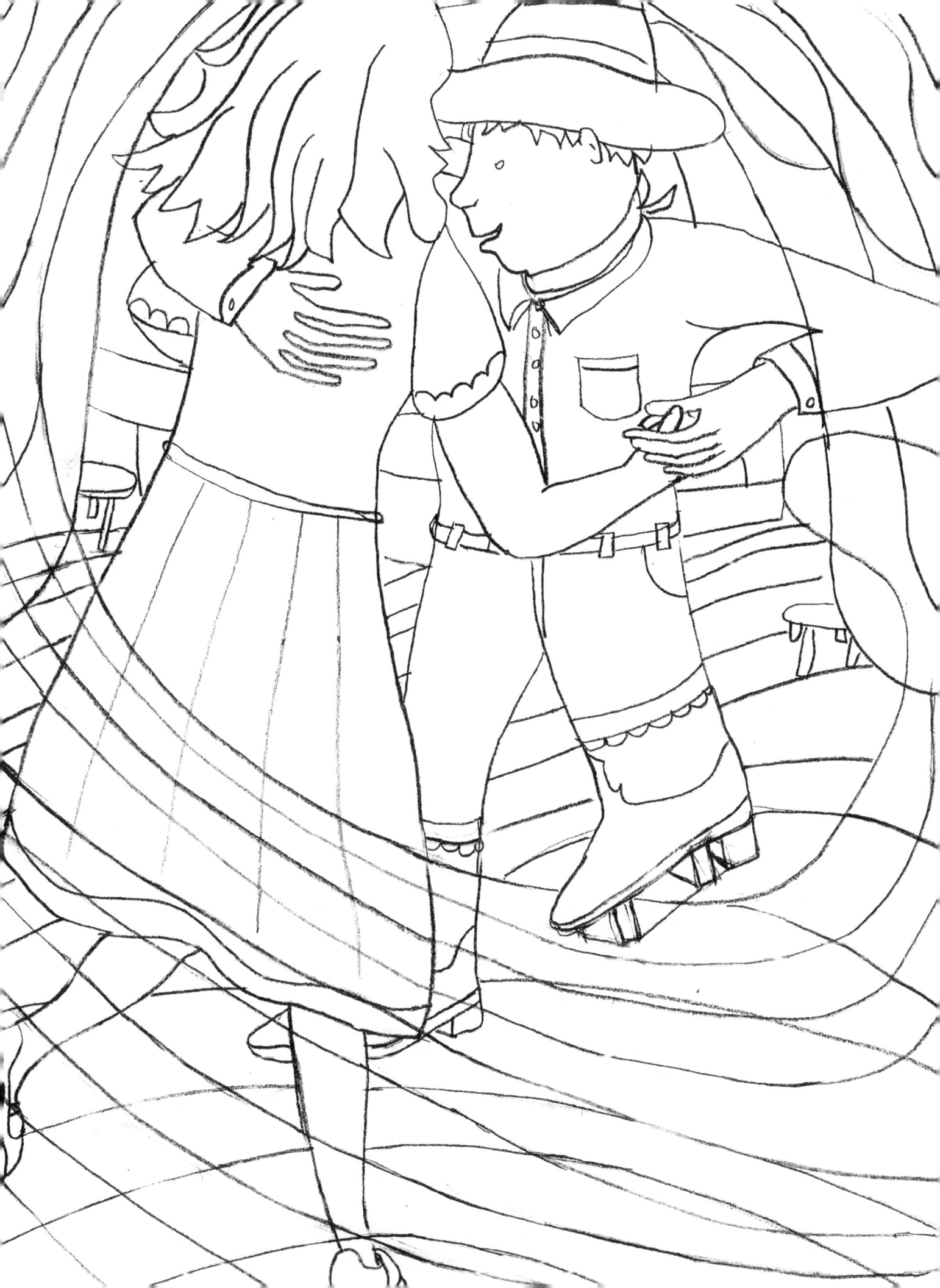

Mary Lawler

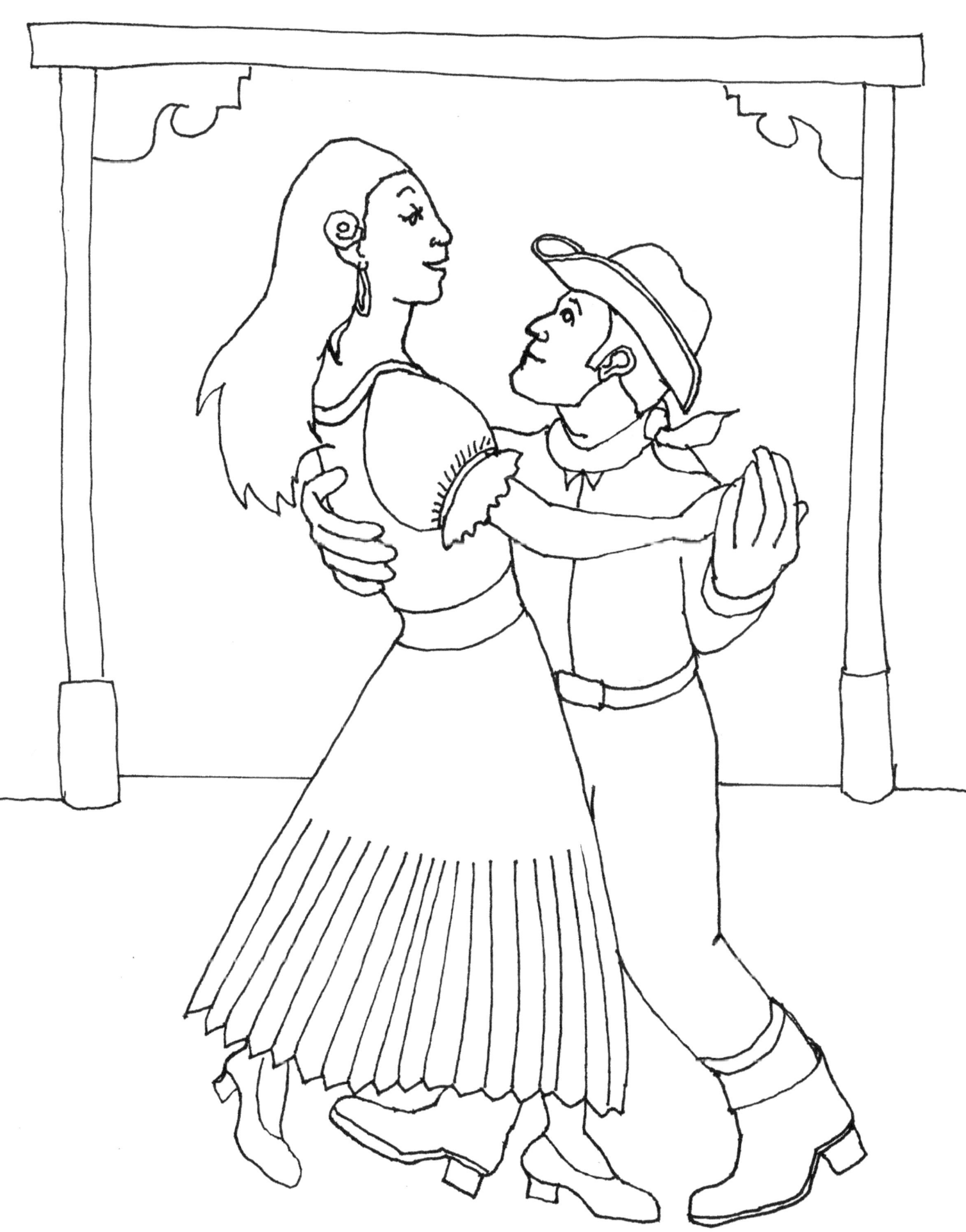

Hye Coh

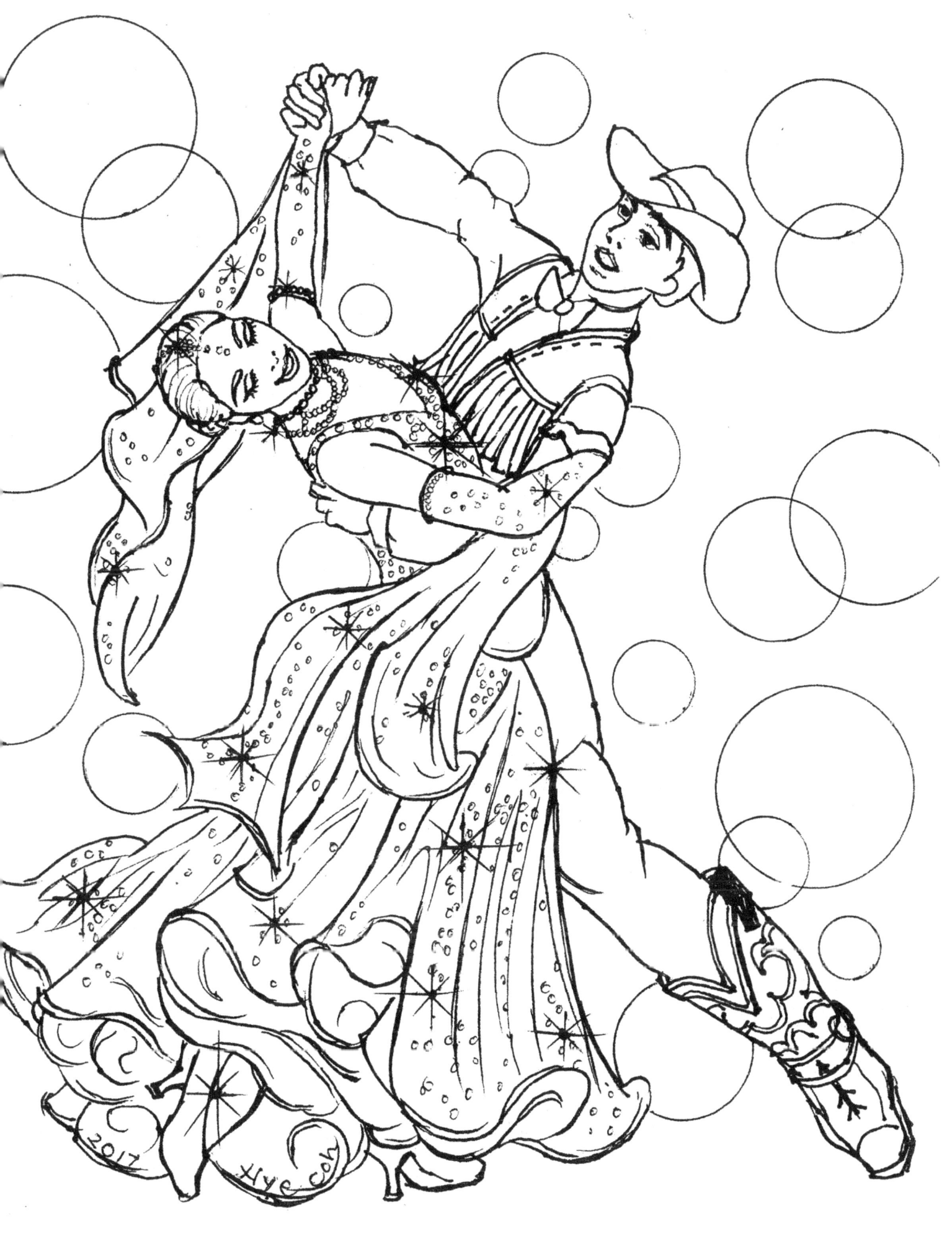

Lisa de St. Croix

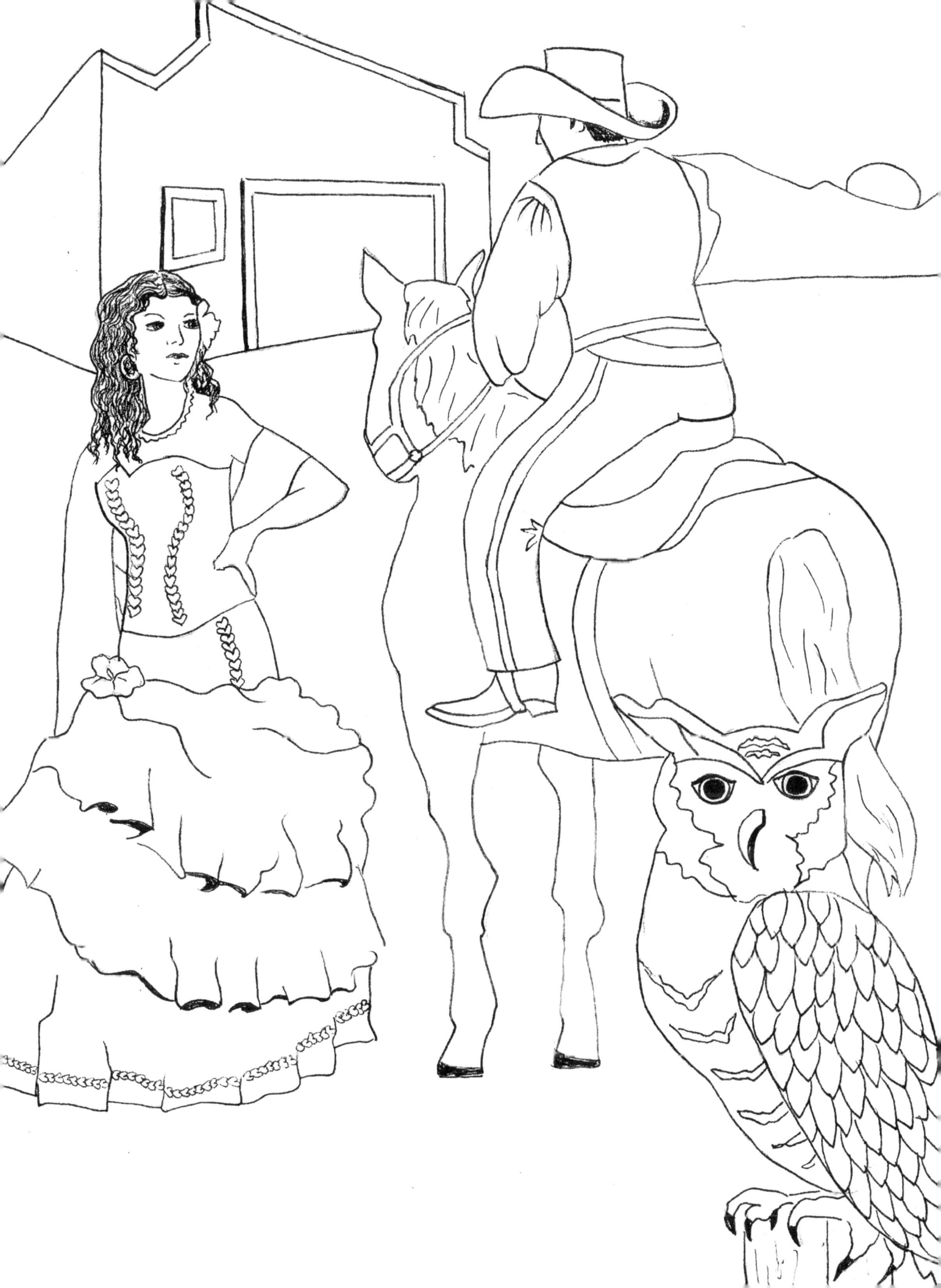

Celeste La Forme

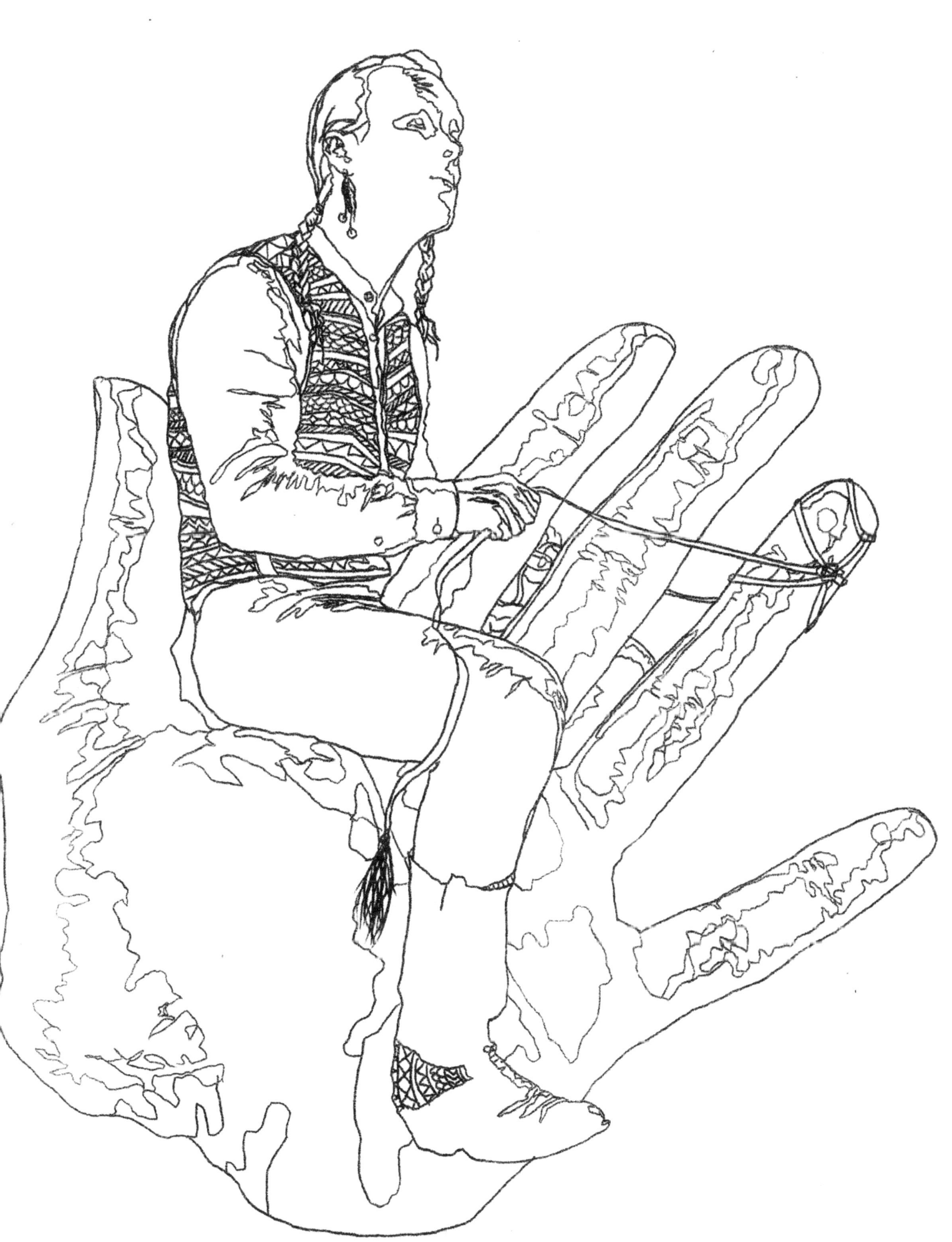

Iren Schio

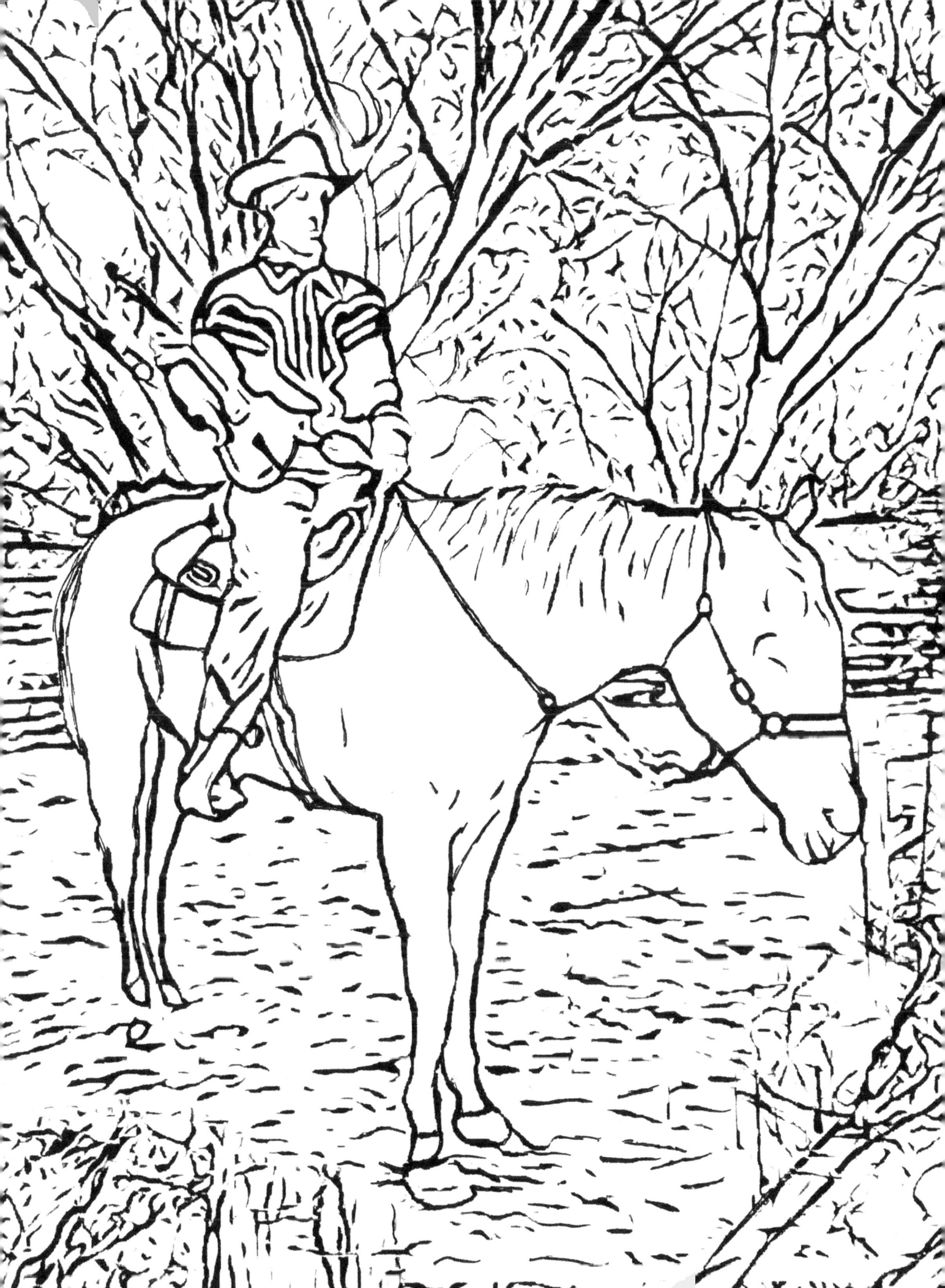

Francesca Yorke

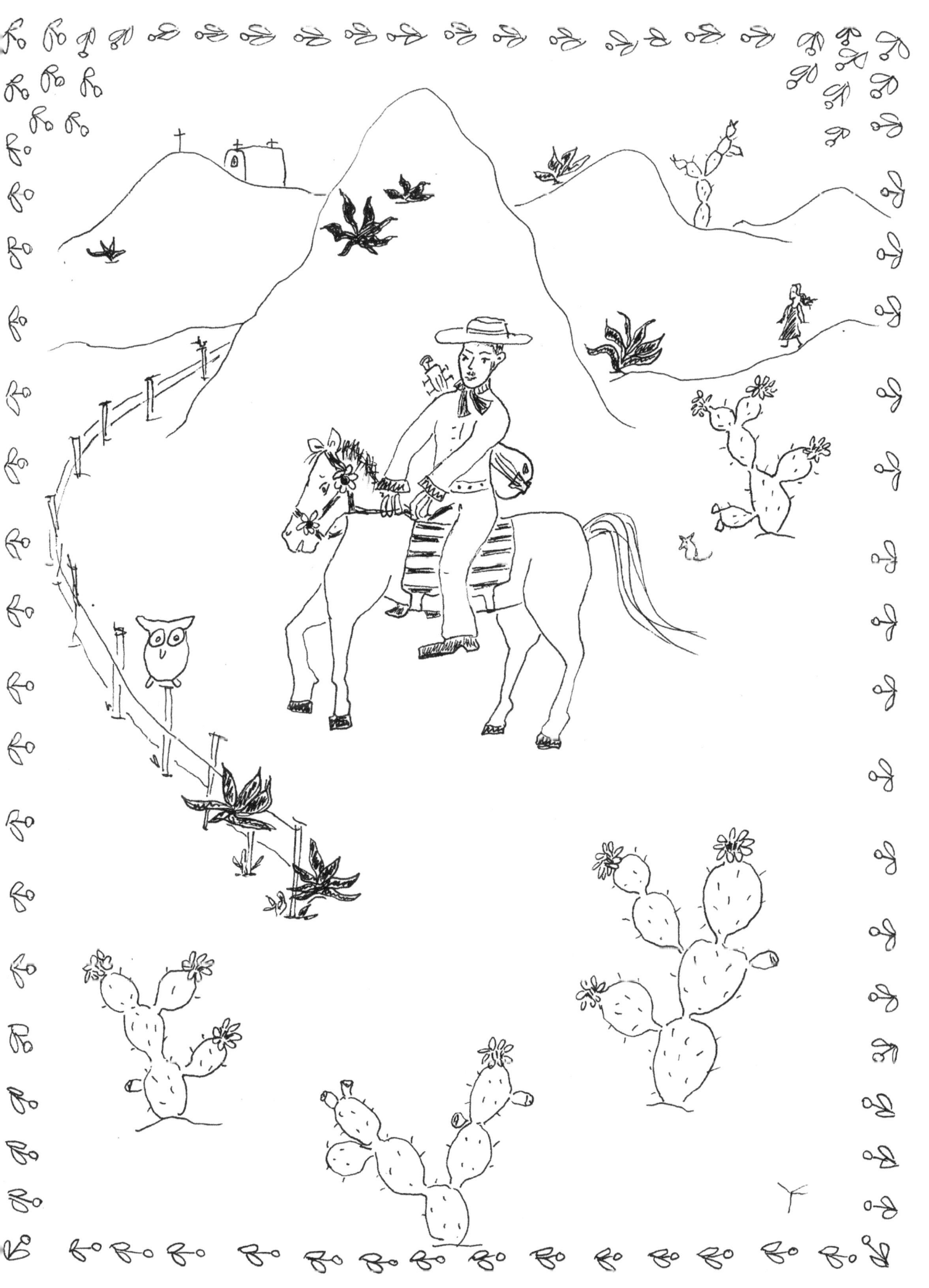

Aidan Mott

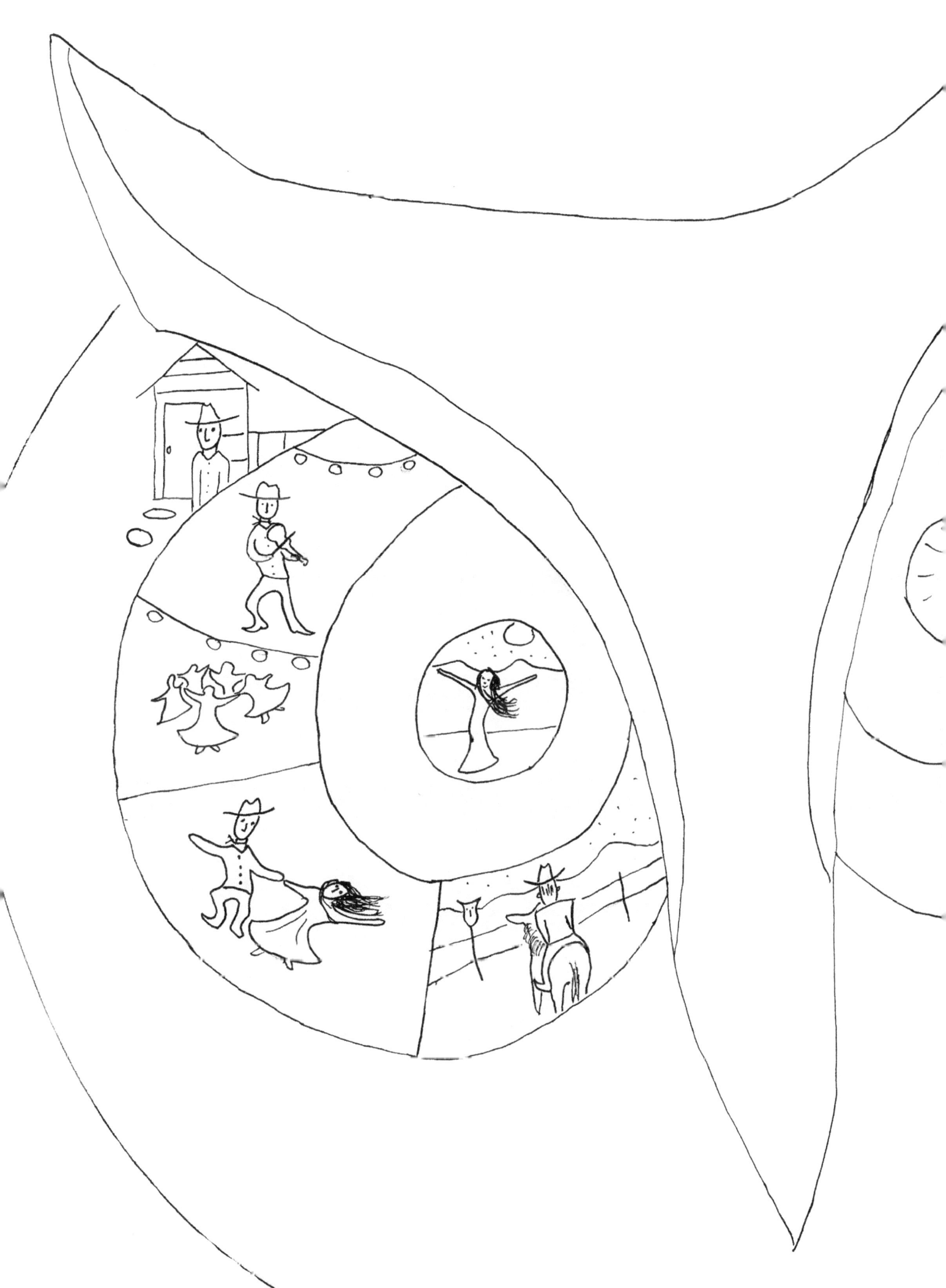

Andrew Fearnside

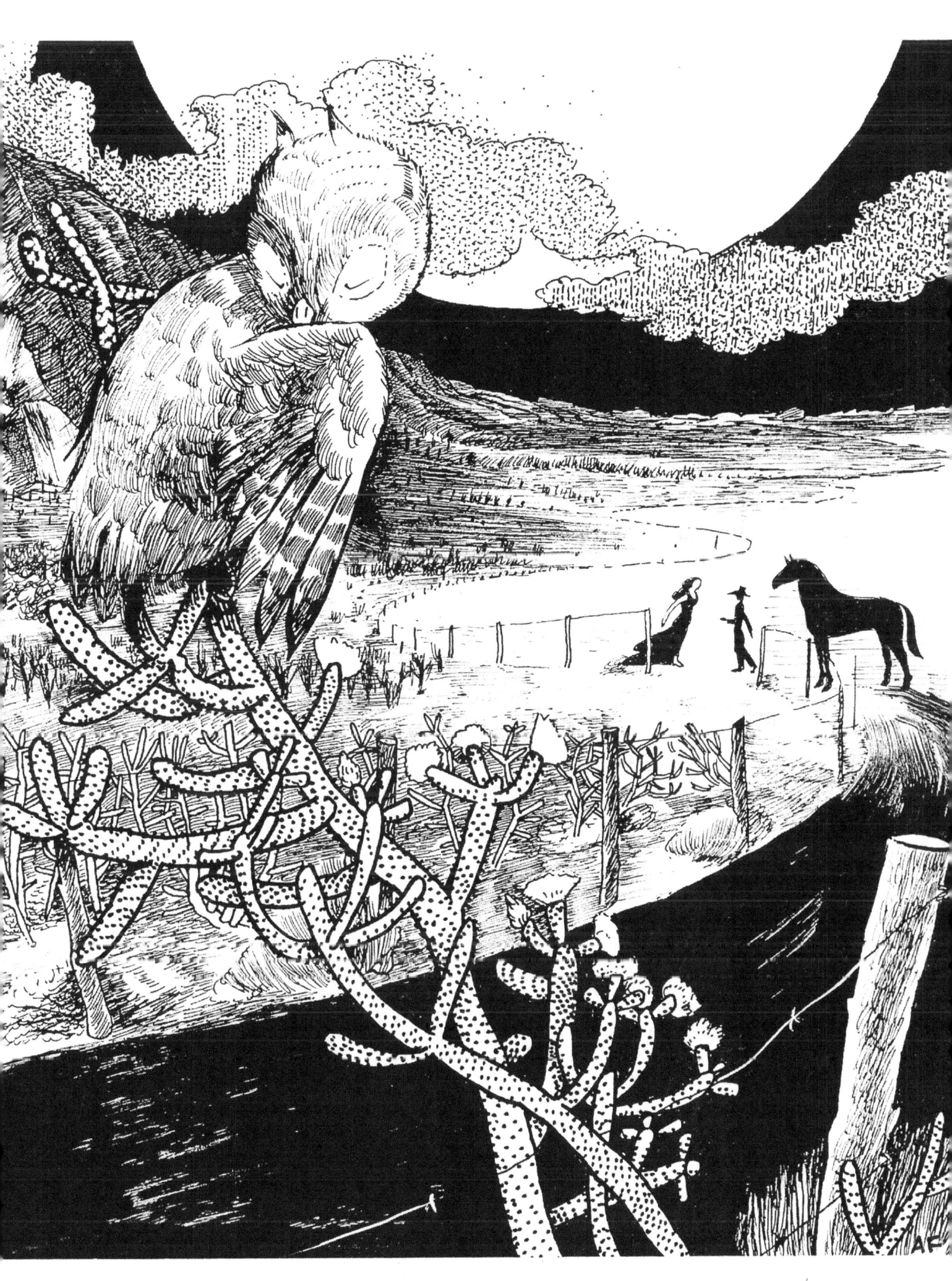

Dancing with a Star

Joe Hayes

One clear winter night when Coyote sat on a ridge top, gazing up at the sky, he saw a beautiful star go dancing clear from the east to the west. The star was so beautiful, and she danced so gracefully across the sky, that Coyote fell in love with her.

Night after night Coyote sat looking up, howling and crying and wishing he could dance in the night with the beautiful star. And then Coyote noticed that in the evening, when the star rose, she danced right by the peak of a mountain far to the east. Coyote decided he would go to the mountaintop and meet the star and ask her if he could dance with her in the sky.

It took Coyote a long time to get to the mountains, and an even longer time to climb to the summit, but late one afternoon he arrived at the very peak of the mountain. He sat waiting for nightfall, and, sure enough, a short while after the sun had set, the star came dancing right by the mountain.

Coyote called out, "Star Maiden, please, let me dance with you in the sky. I have been watching you every night. I think you are the most beautiful and the most graceful star in the sky."

The star maiden reached her hand down and took hold of Coyote's hand. They danced together into the sky. Coyote lifted his knees high and whirled in circles as danced. He felt as though all his dreams had come true.

But the star maiden danced clear from the east to the west in just one night, so she had to dance fast. And she wouldn't stop to rest, not even for a minute, all night long!

By the time they were a quarter of the way across the sky, Coyote was puffing and panting and dripping with sweat, but he swore to himself he would dance with the star all night long.

But… by the time they reached the top of the sky, Coyote was so tired he couldn't pick up his feet anymore. He couldn't hold his head high. He couldn't even hang onto the star maiden's hand!

Coyote let go. And he fell! He fell through the sky so fast that he burned up in a flash of white light!

The other animals saw the flash. Some of them said, "That foolish Coyote! Who does he think he is, trying to dance with a star? He got just what he deserved. He should have stayed down here on the ground where he belongs."

But other animals disagreed. "No," they said. "At least Coyote tried to do the one thing his heart was longing to do. It was better for him to dance half-way across the sky with the star, and then fall to earth in a flash of fire, than to spend the rest of his life sitting on the ground crying and wishing he could dance with a star. And, besides, didn't Coyote make a beautiful light when he fell?"

So, if you ever happen to be outside on a clear winter night and you see a shooting star go flashing across the sky, think about Coyote. And then decide: Was Coyote a fool, or was he sort of a hero, because he tried to dance with a star?

Brian Fleetwood

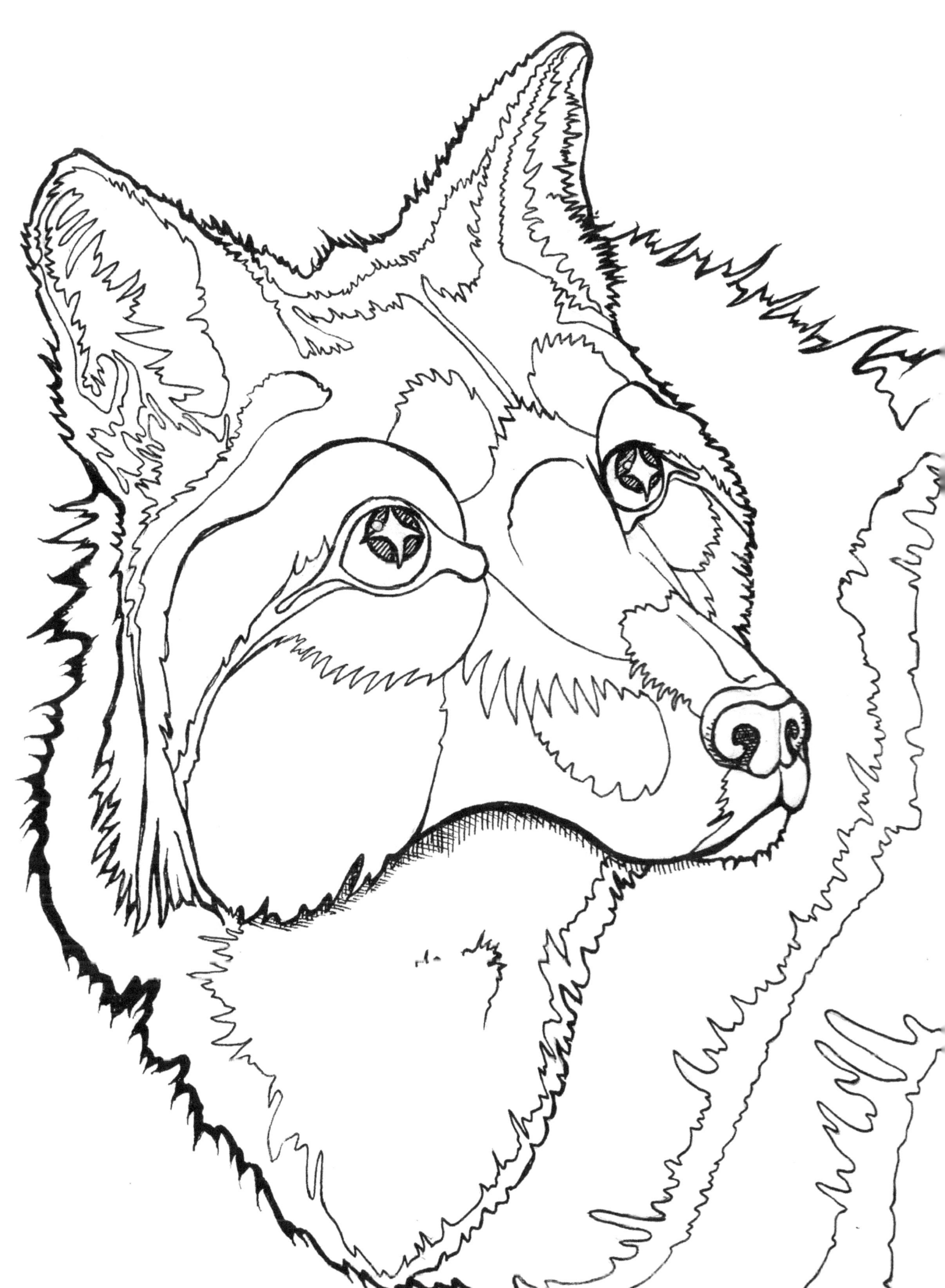

Linda Guenste

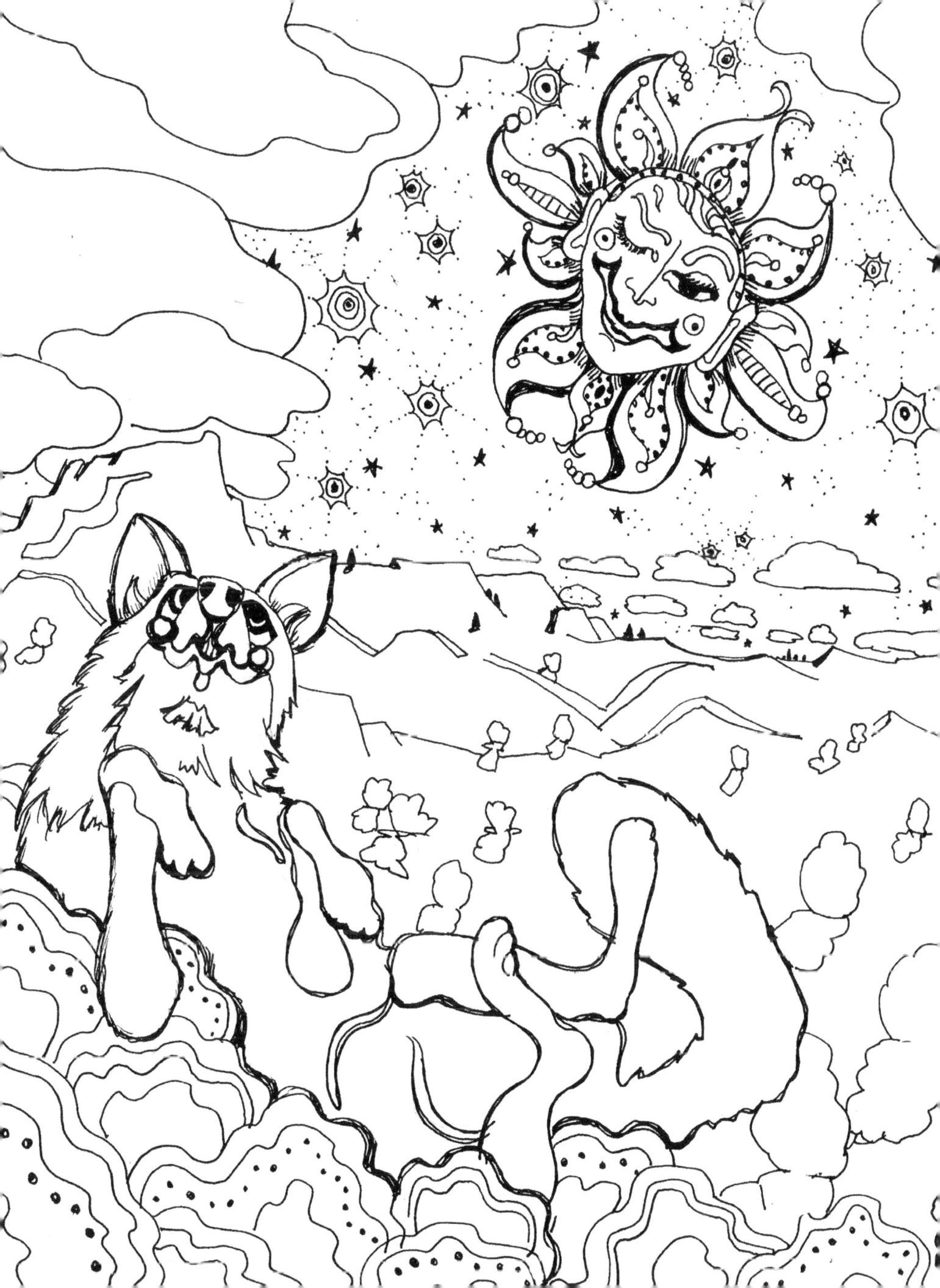

Tricia Tusa

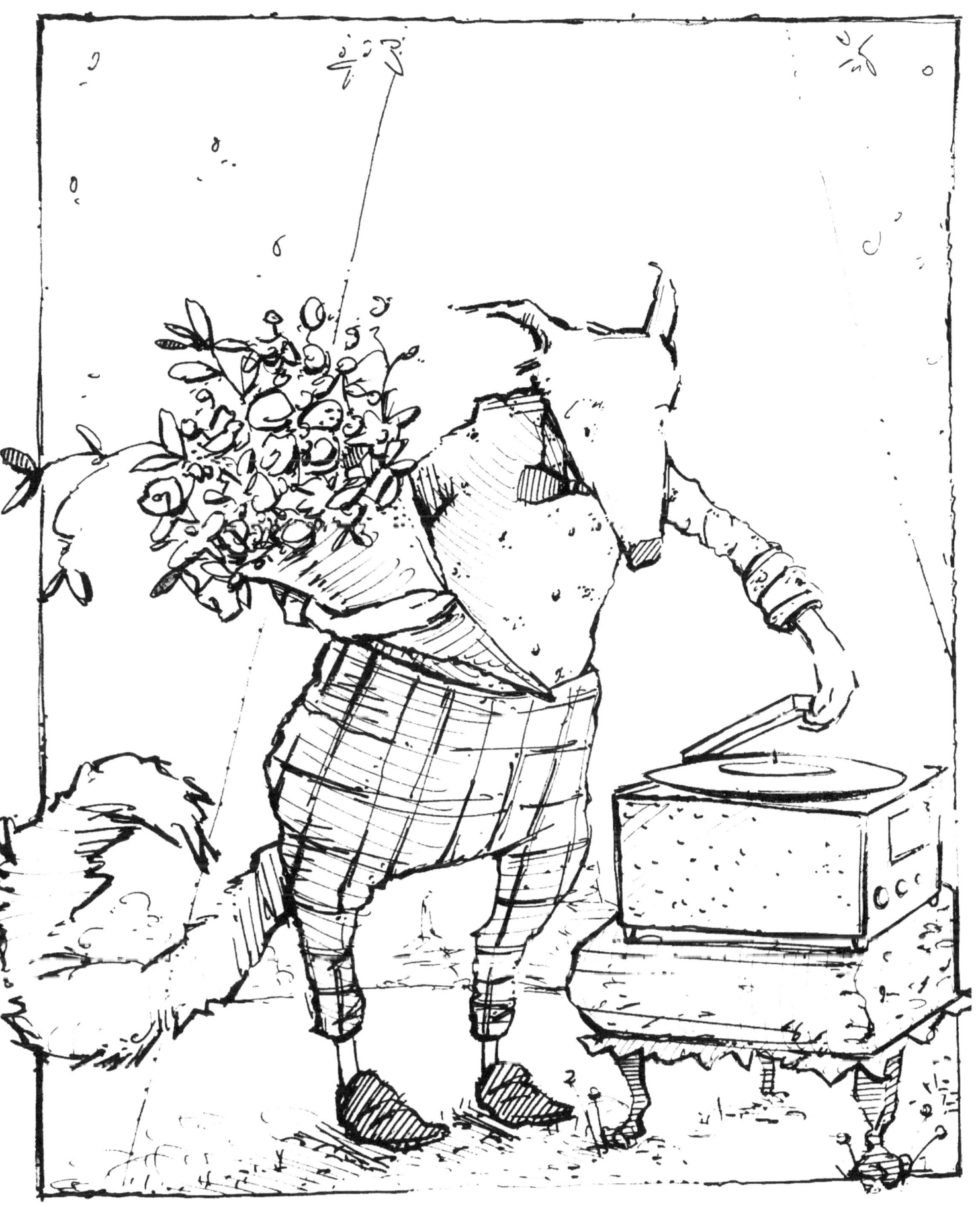

Mikey Rae

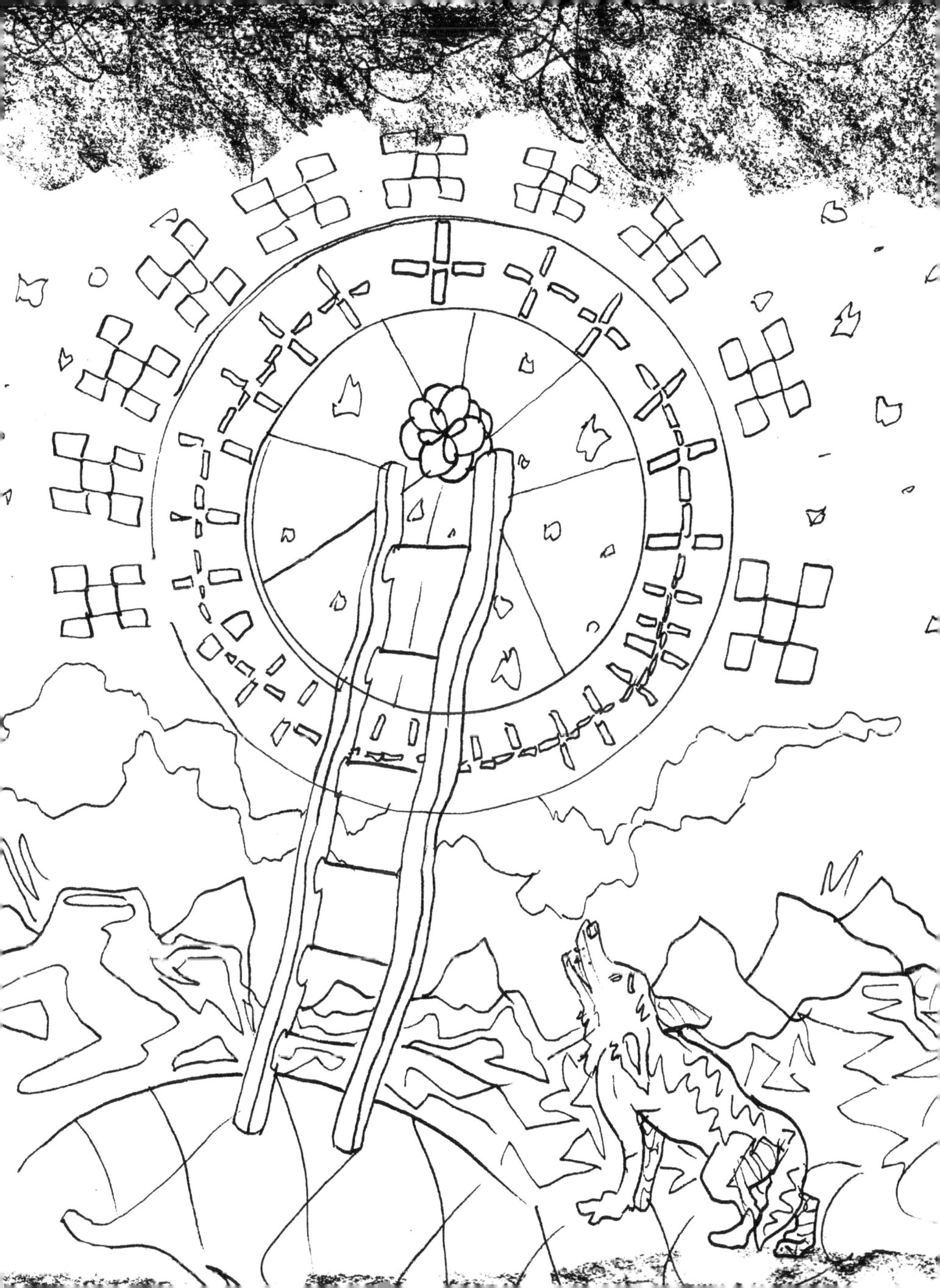

Susan Case

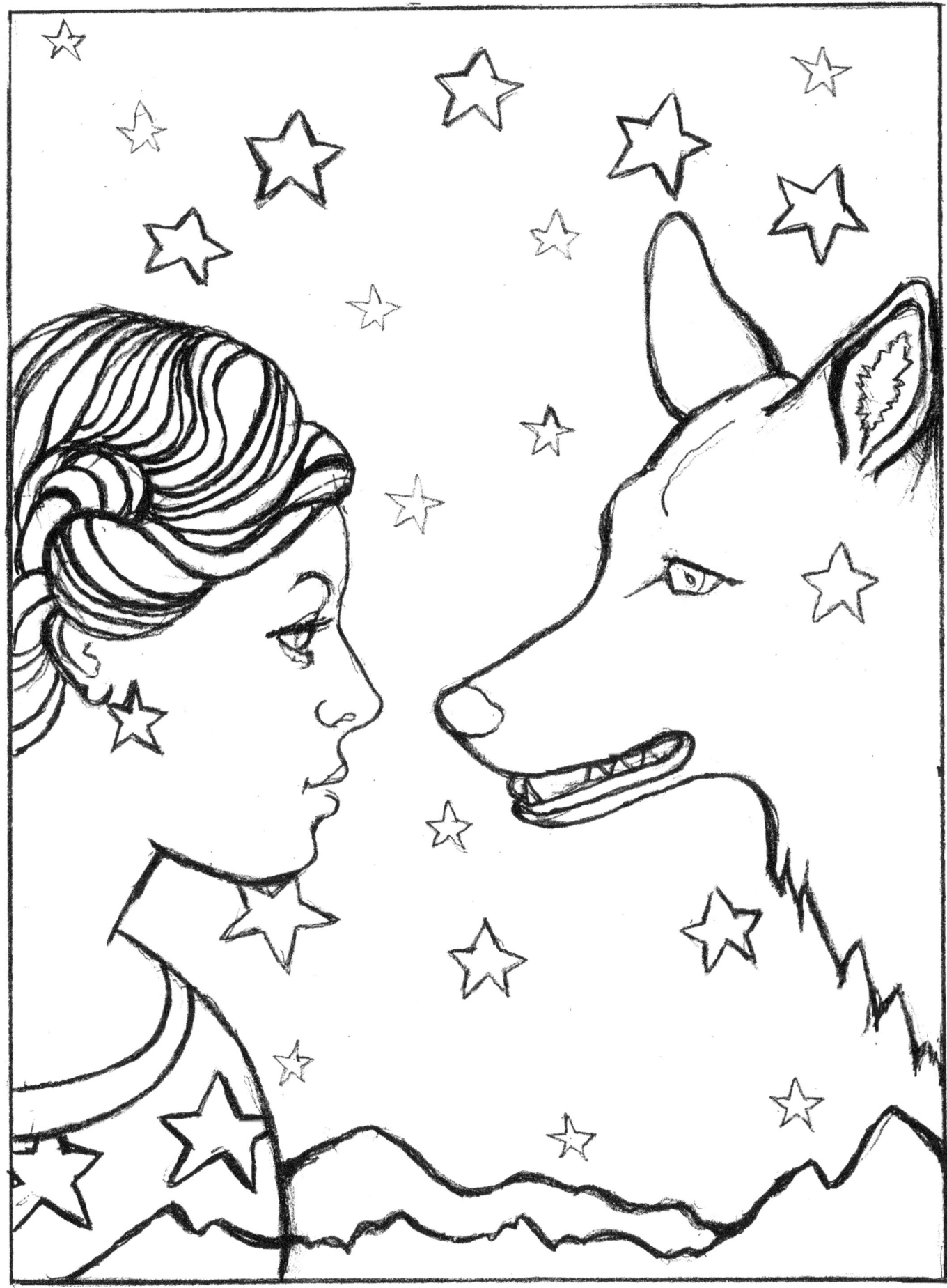

Donelli J. DiMaria

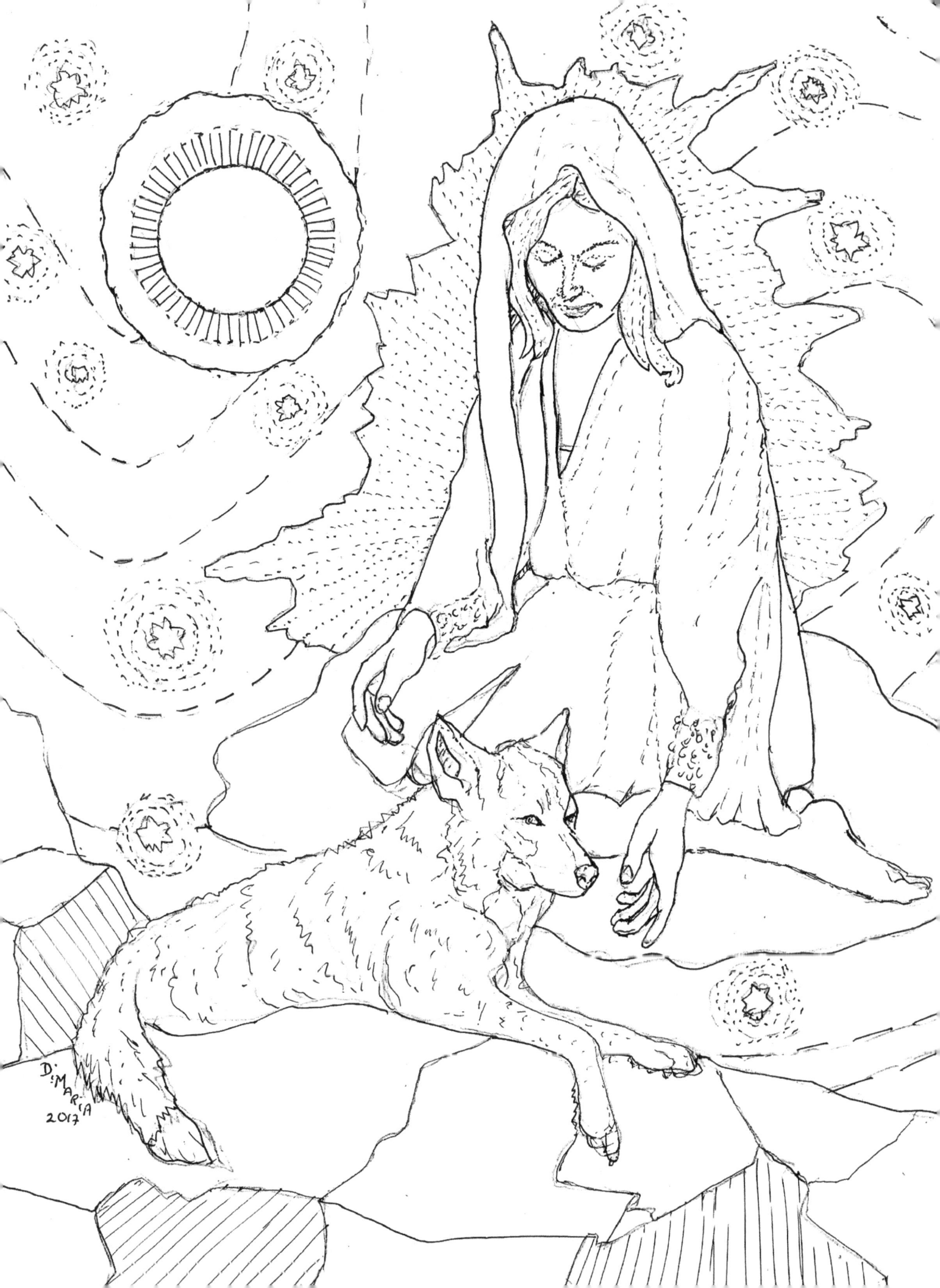

Abby Mattison

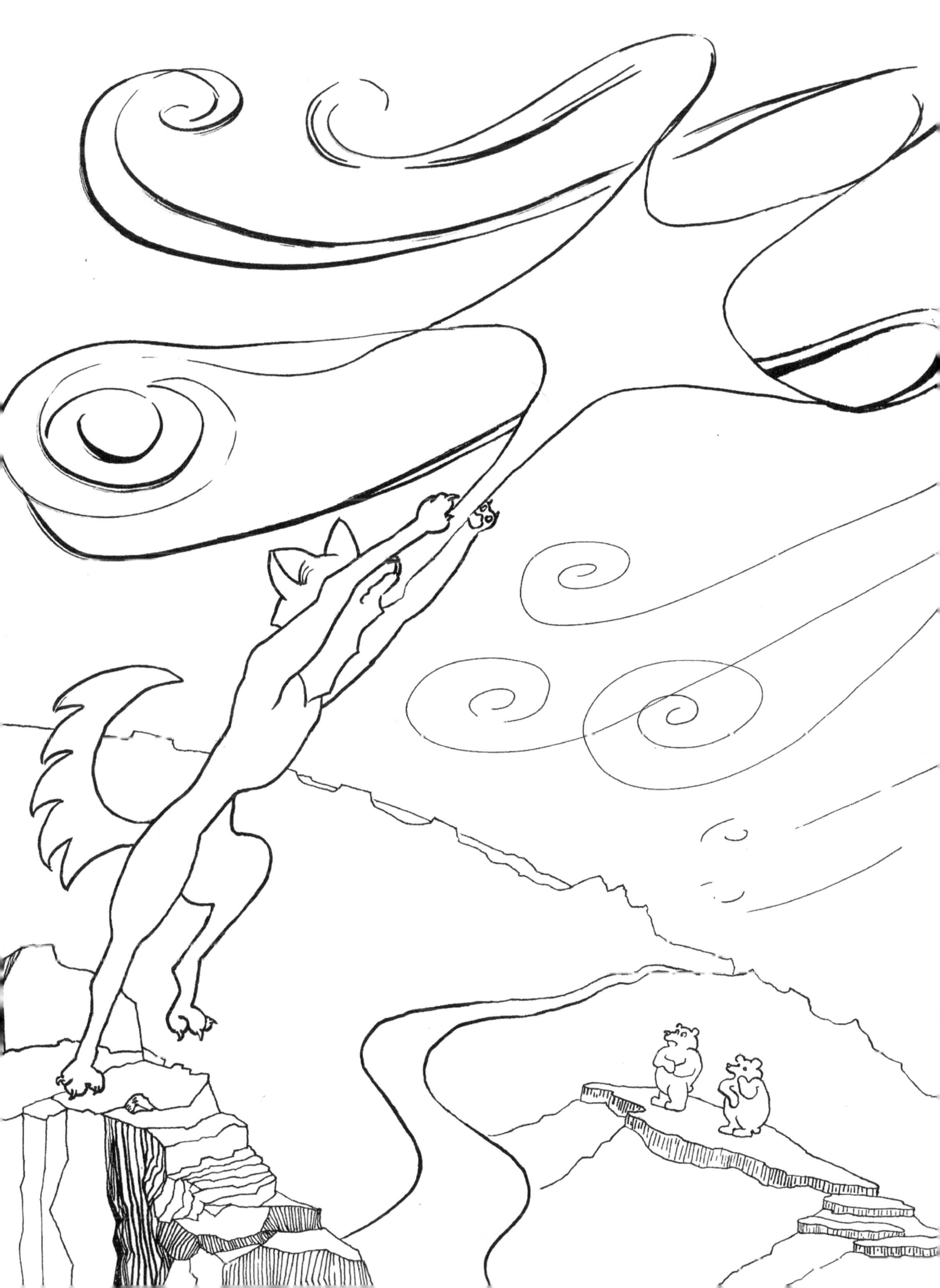

Betsy Emil

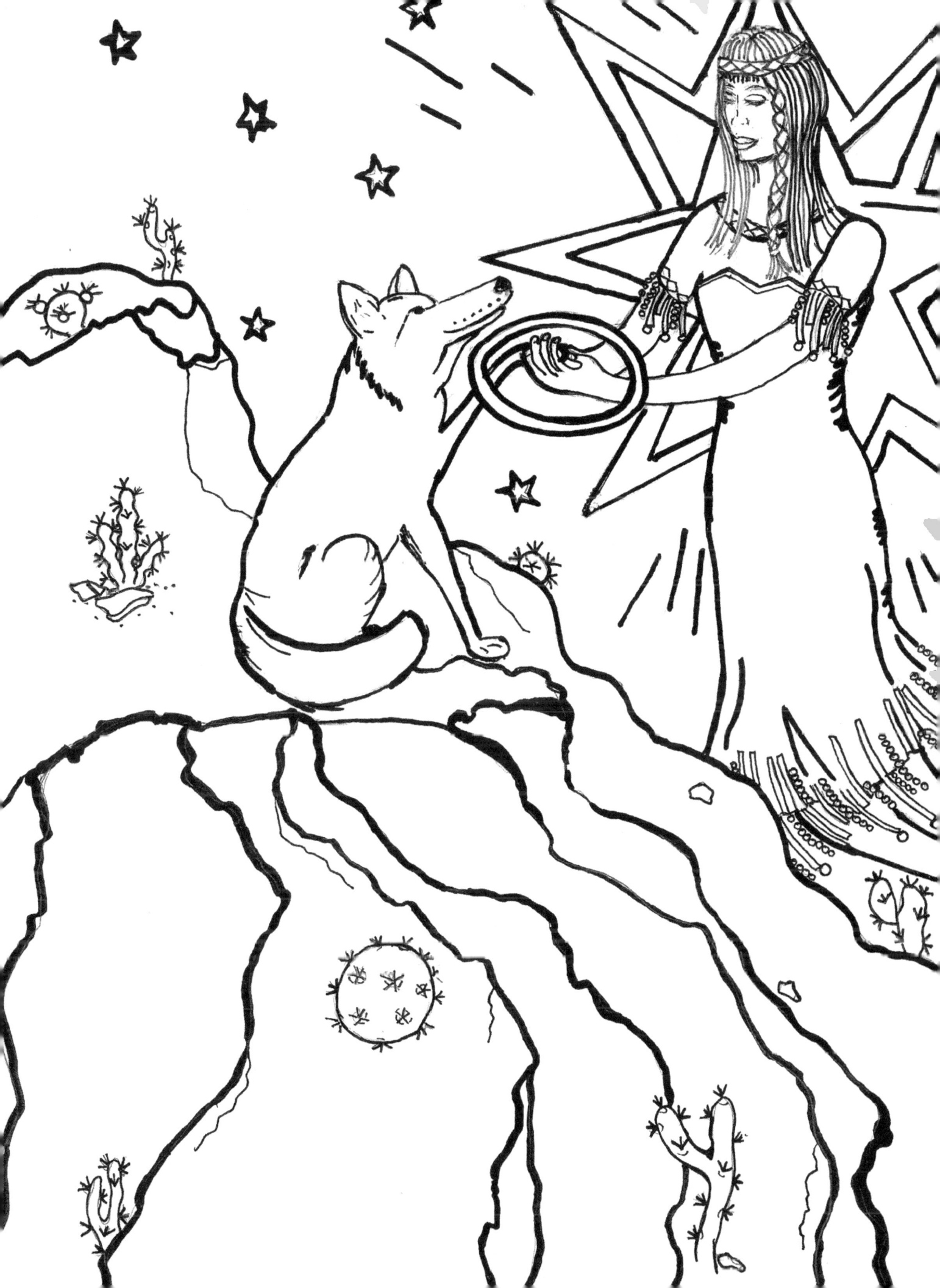

Debby Young

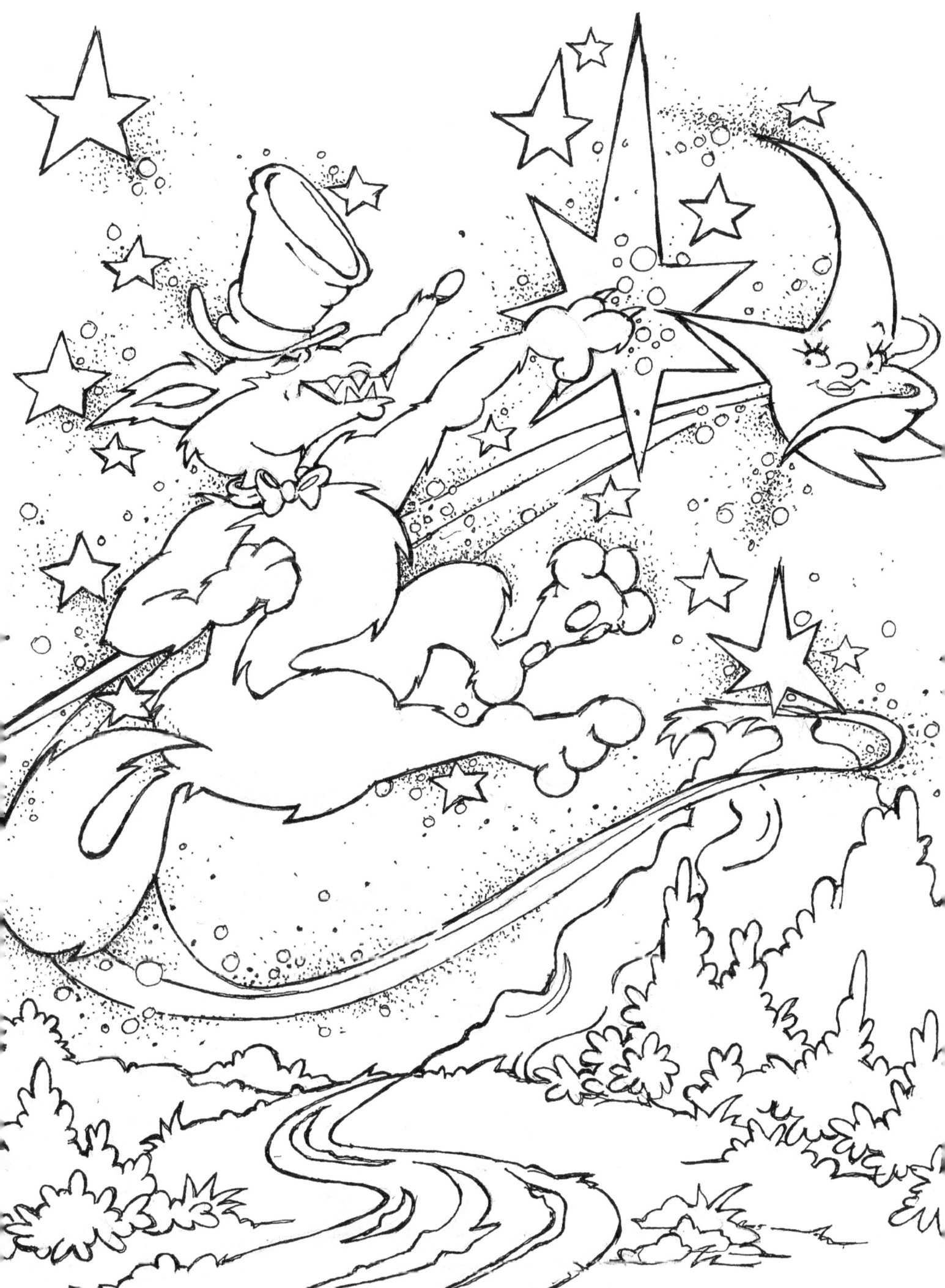

Erin Currier

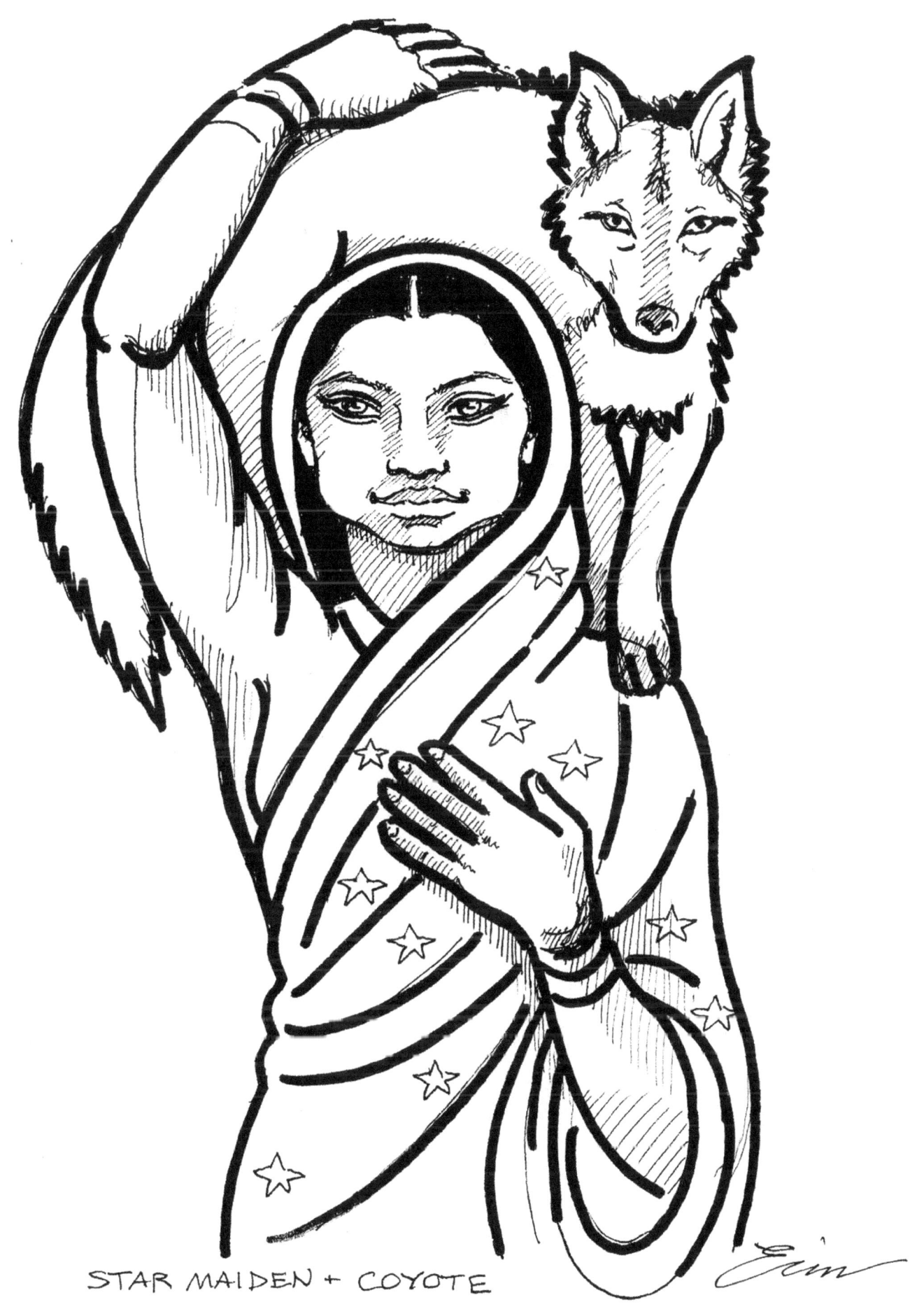

STAR MAIDEN + COYOTE

William Rotseart

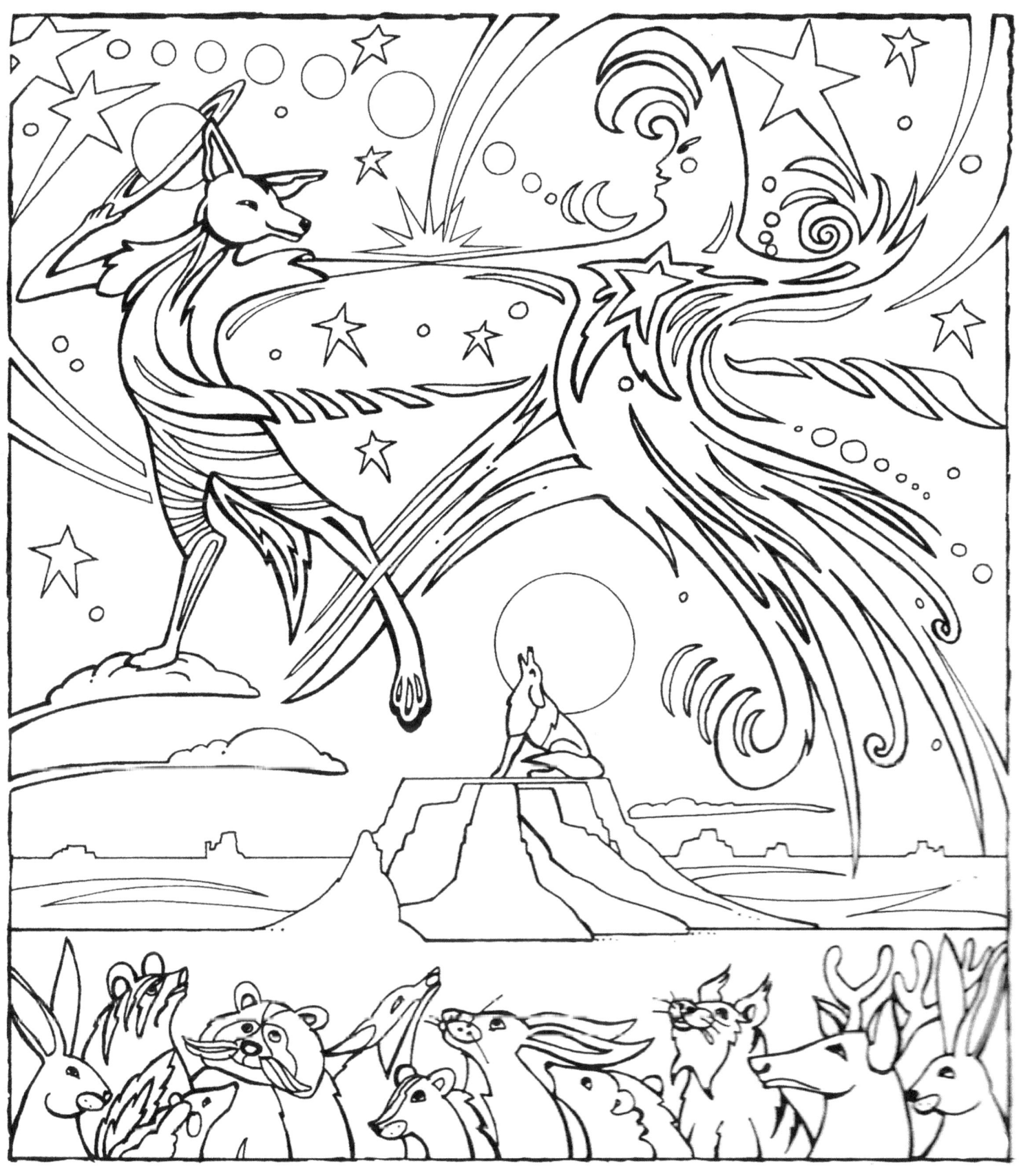

Janet Stein Romero

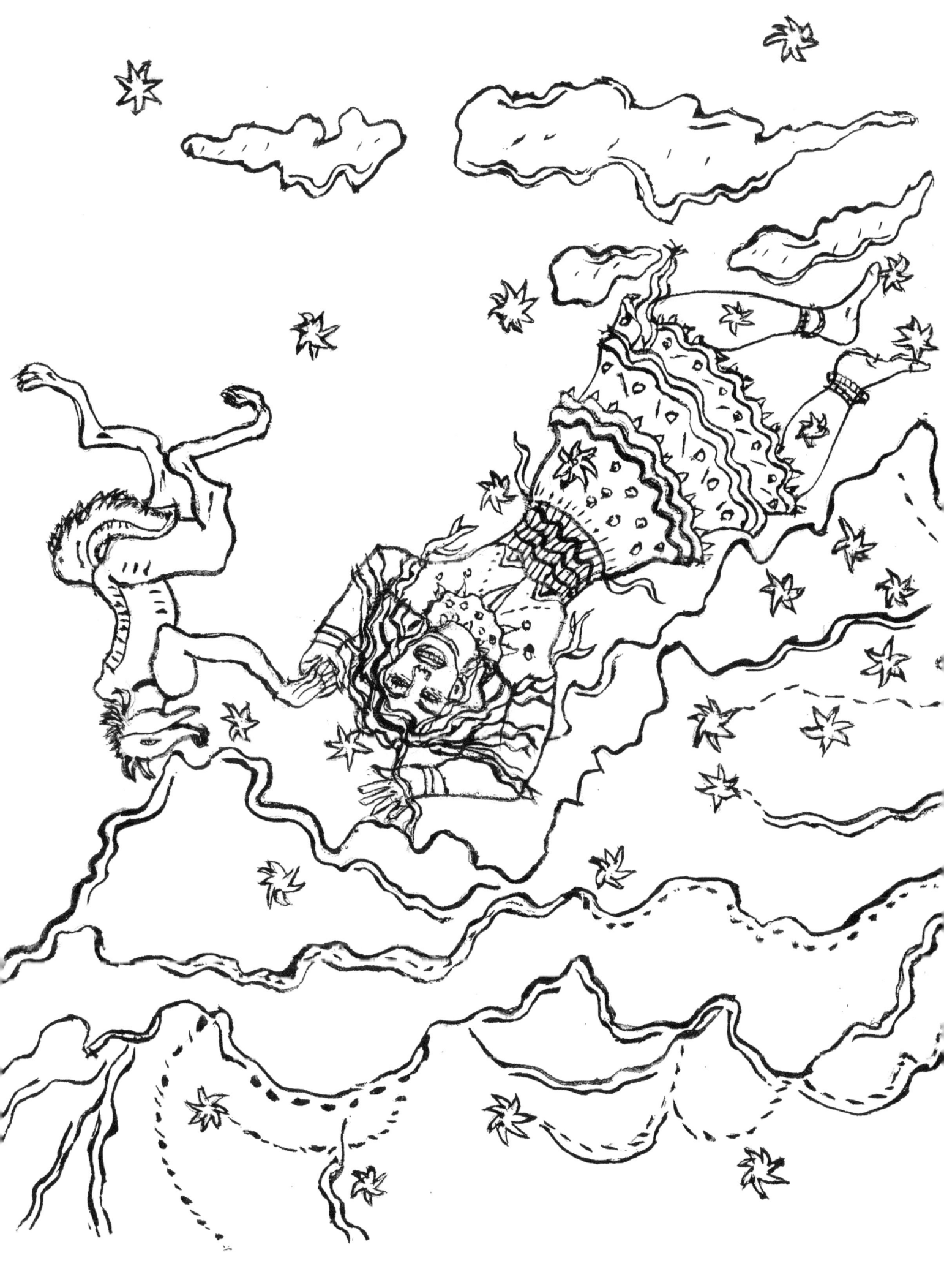

Sabra Moore

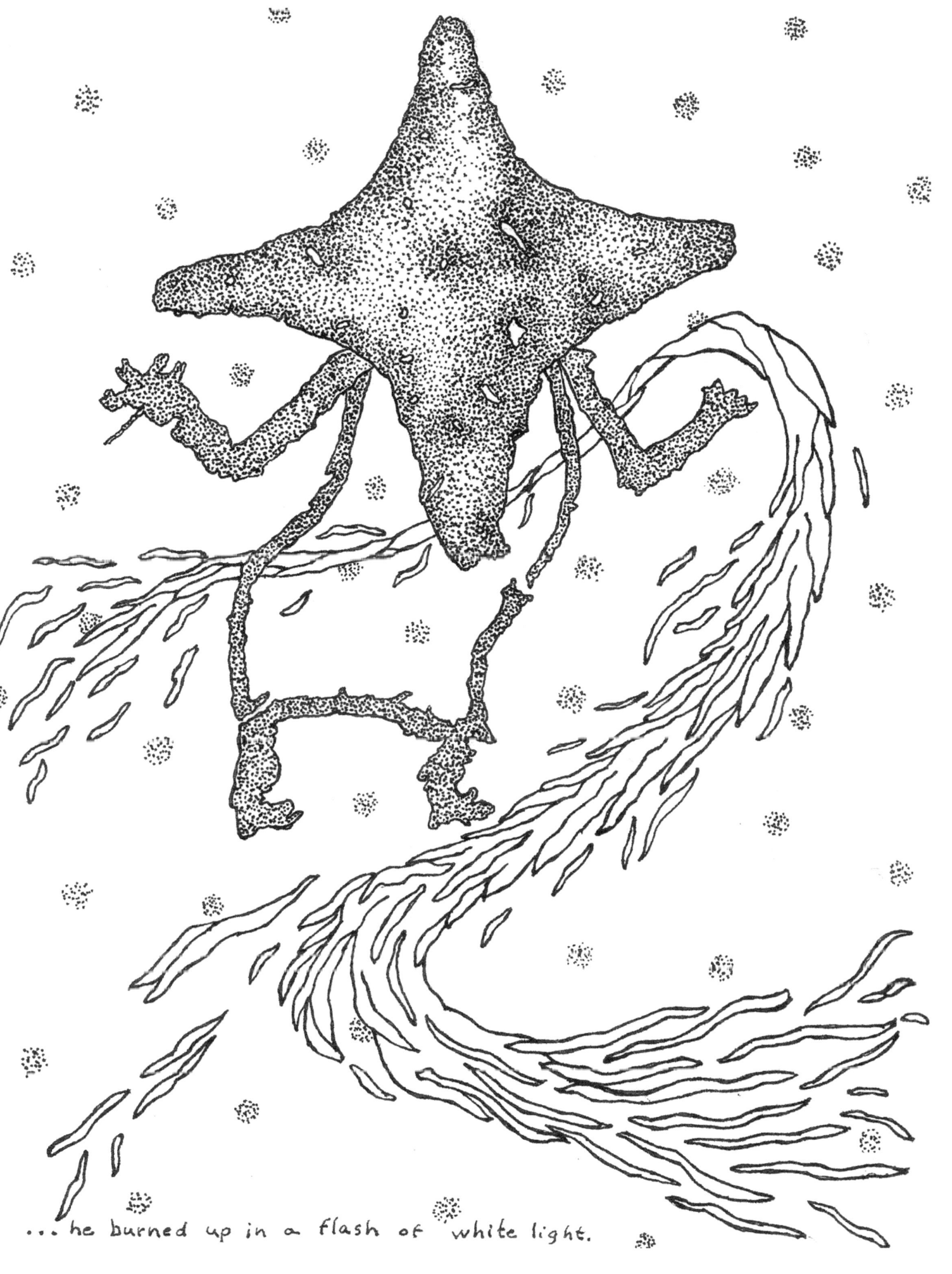

...he burned up in a flash of white light.

Miranda Gray

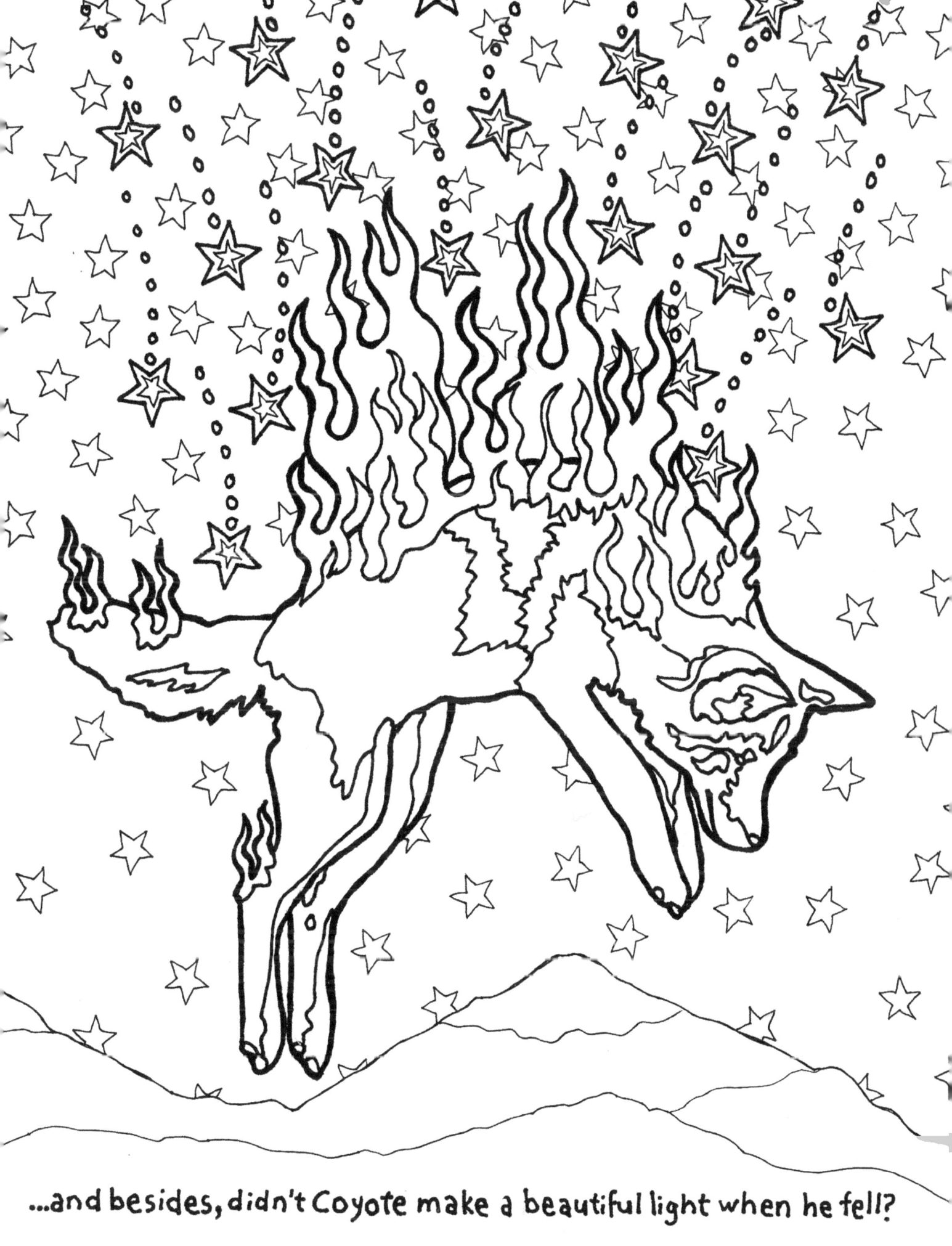

...and besides, didn't Coyote make a beautiful light when he fell?

Two Stories

Lily Hoang

Silent Night with Ten Billion Falling Raindrops

Outside, there is a monsoon huffing around the desert. Rain rumbles like nightmares, and there is not a person in sight. Everyone is hiding inside adobe, telling fairy stories about princesses and frogs and all sorts of funny animals.

Tonight, not a single soul knocks on any door—save the ghouls and monsters—and little girls and little boys should know better than to open their doors to such malicious creatures, even if it is impolite behavior, especially on a night like tonight. On a night like tonight, we might even pity the devil, but we shan't! No, we are wiser than that.

But beware of windows, always beware of those windows.

On Wooden Interrogations

Who knocks on doors anymore? Only the truly gentle, that's who— there are no more princes or gentlemen or kindness left in the world, merely brutes and giants who kick in doors or pound them into feathery splinters, even devils are too polite to raise a single disturbing fist.

Aaron Yazzie

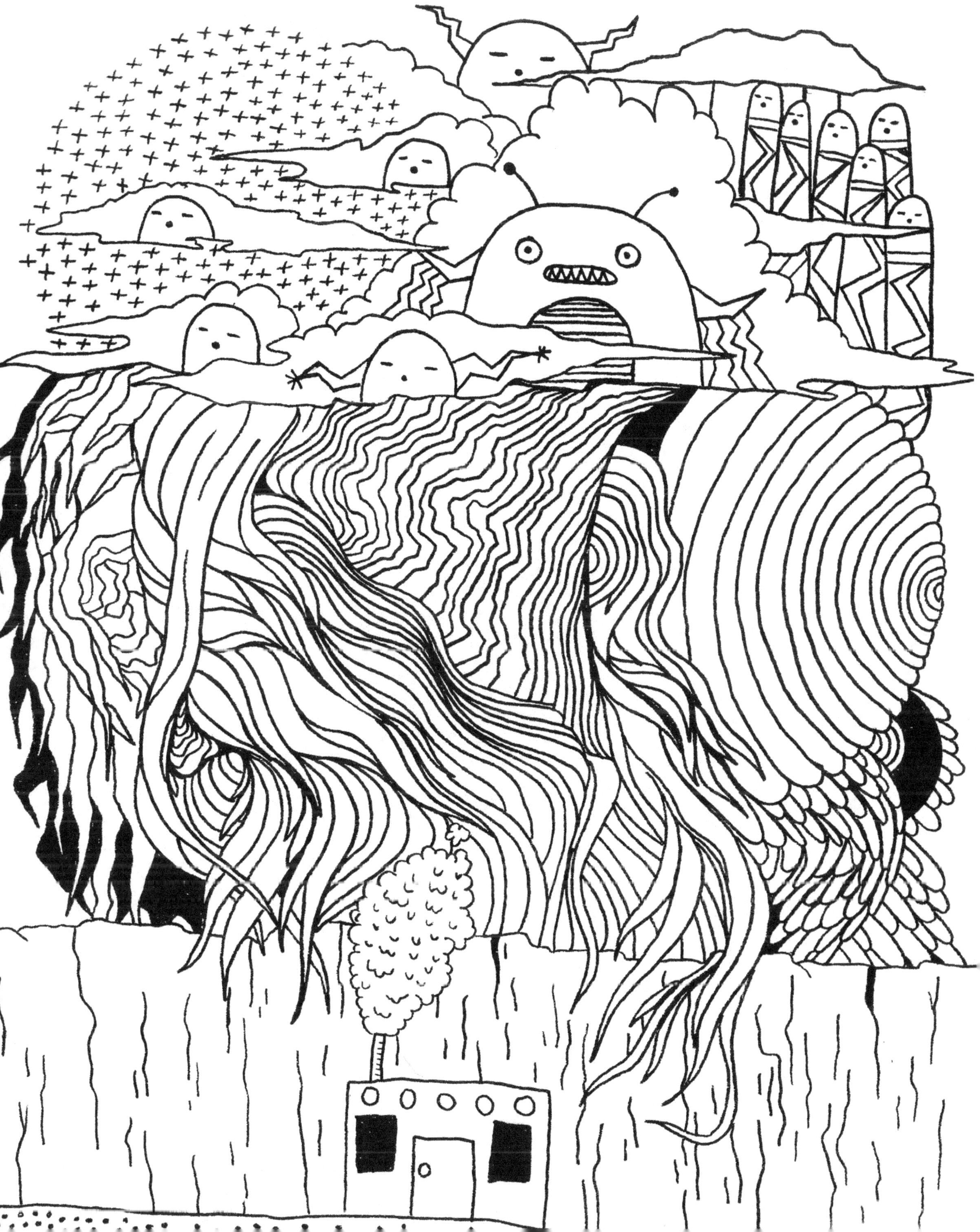

Mark Spencer

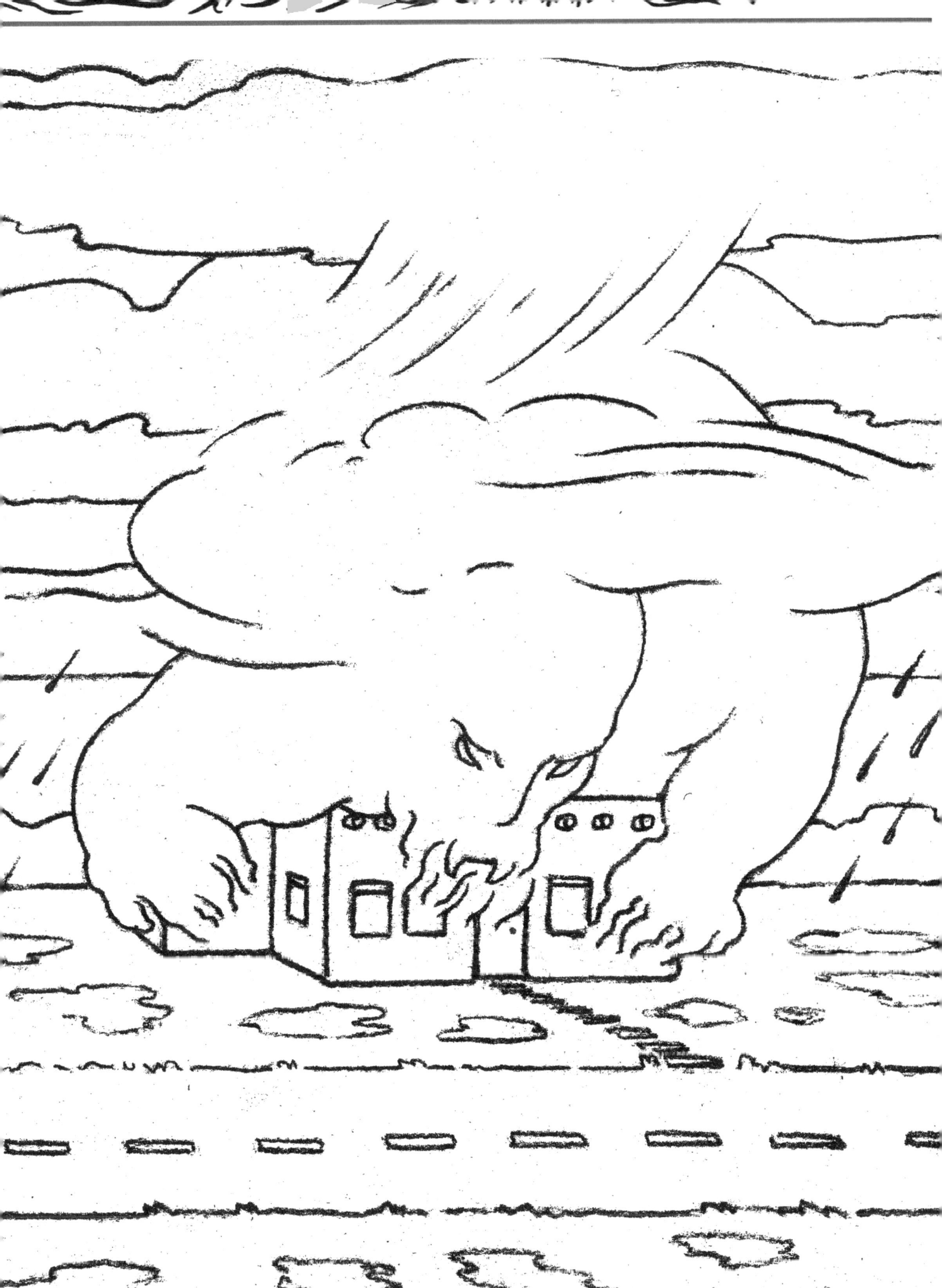

Jeff Benham

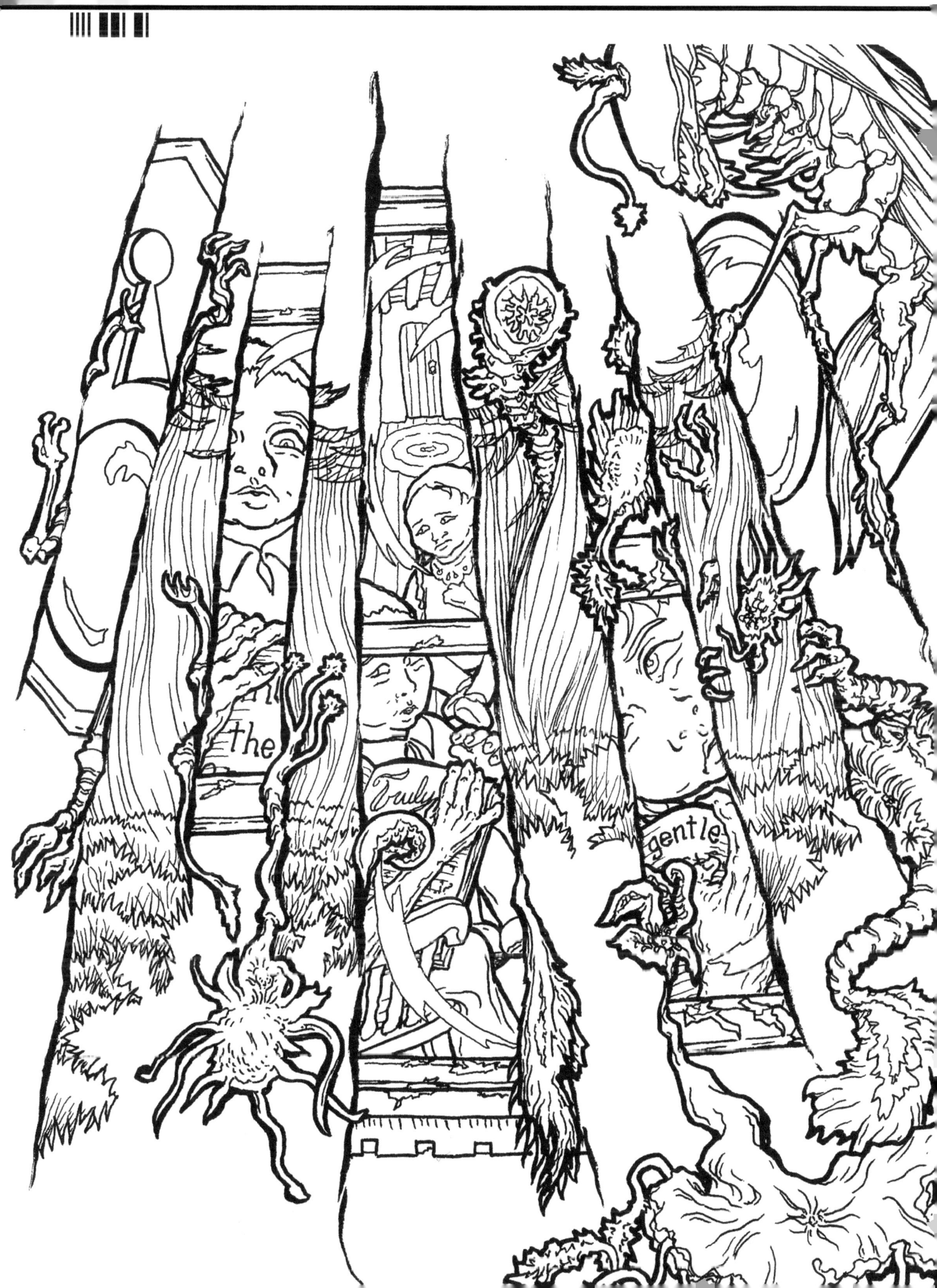

Victoria Carlson

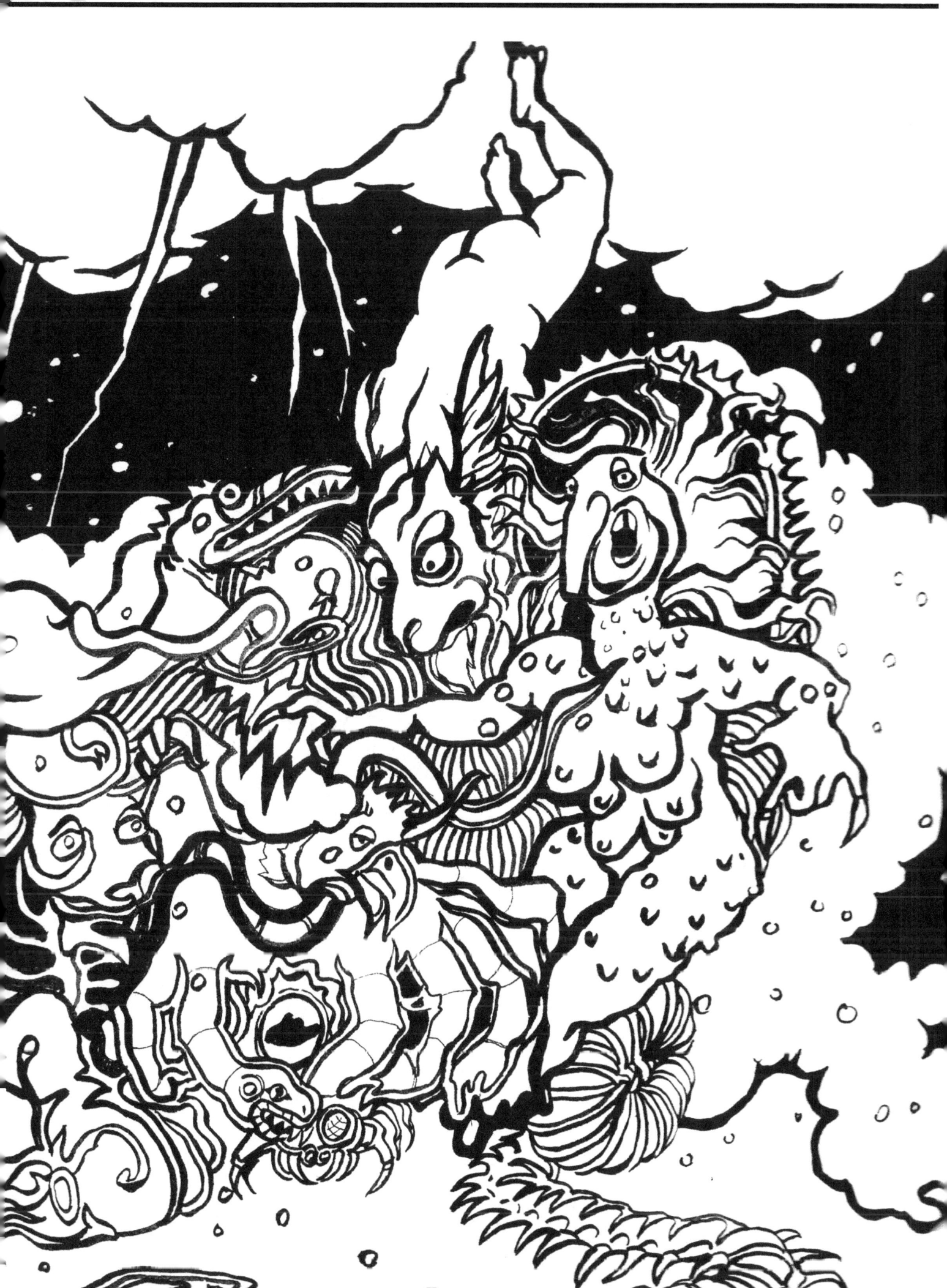

Matthew Chase-Daniel

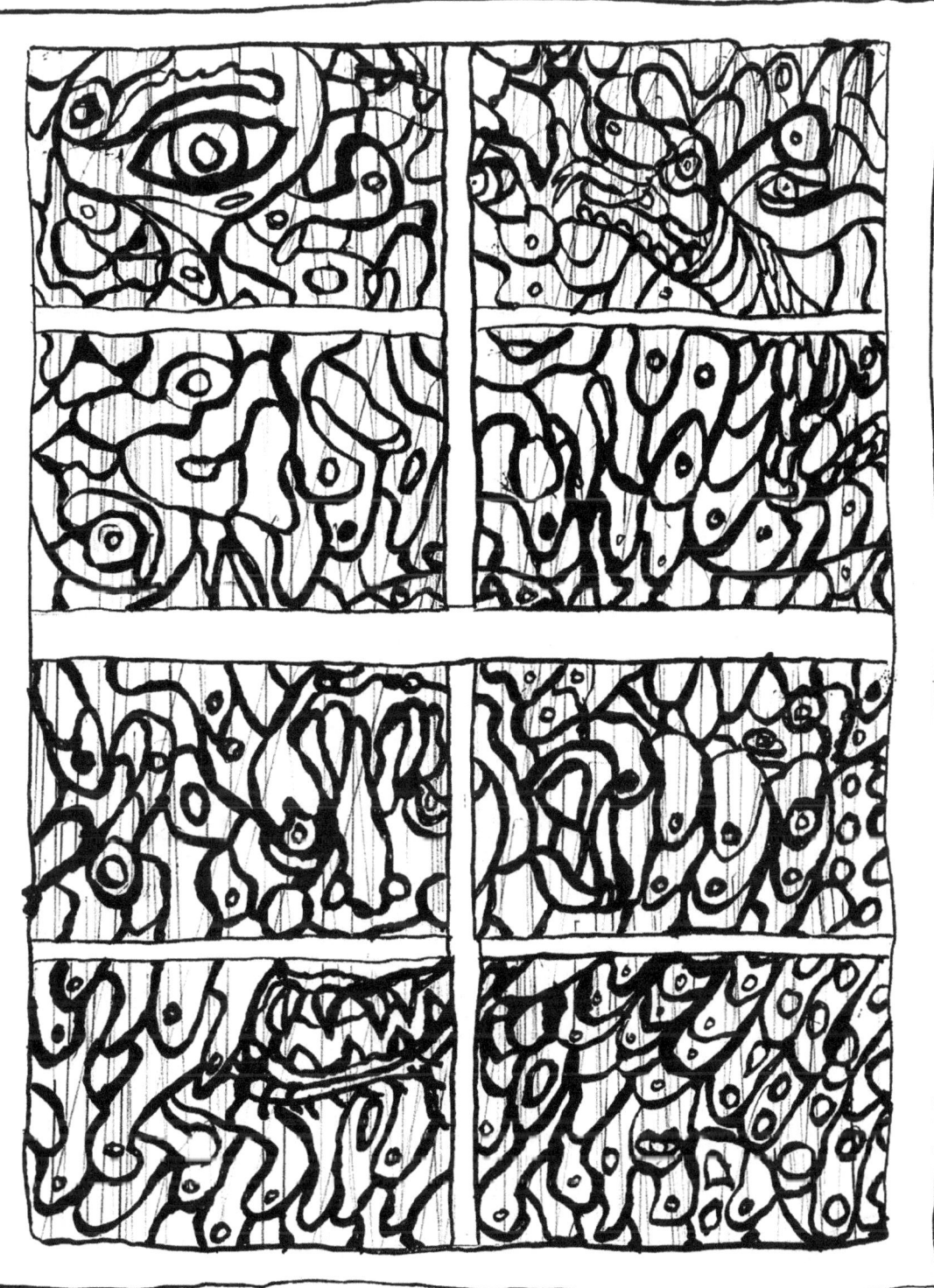

Nicola Heindl-Watson

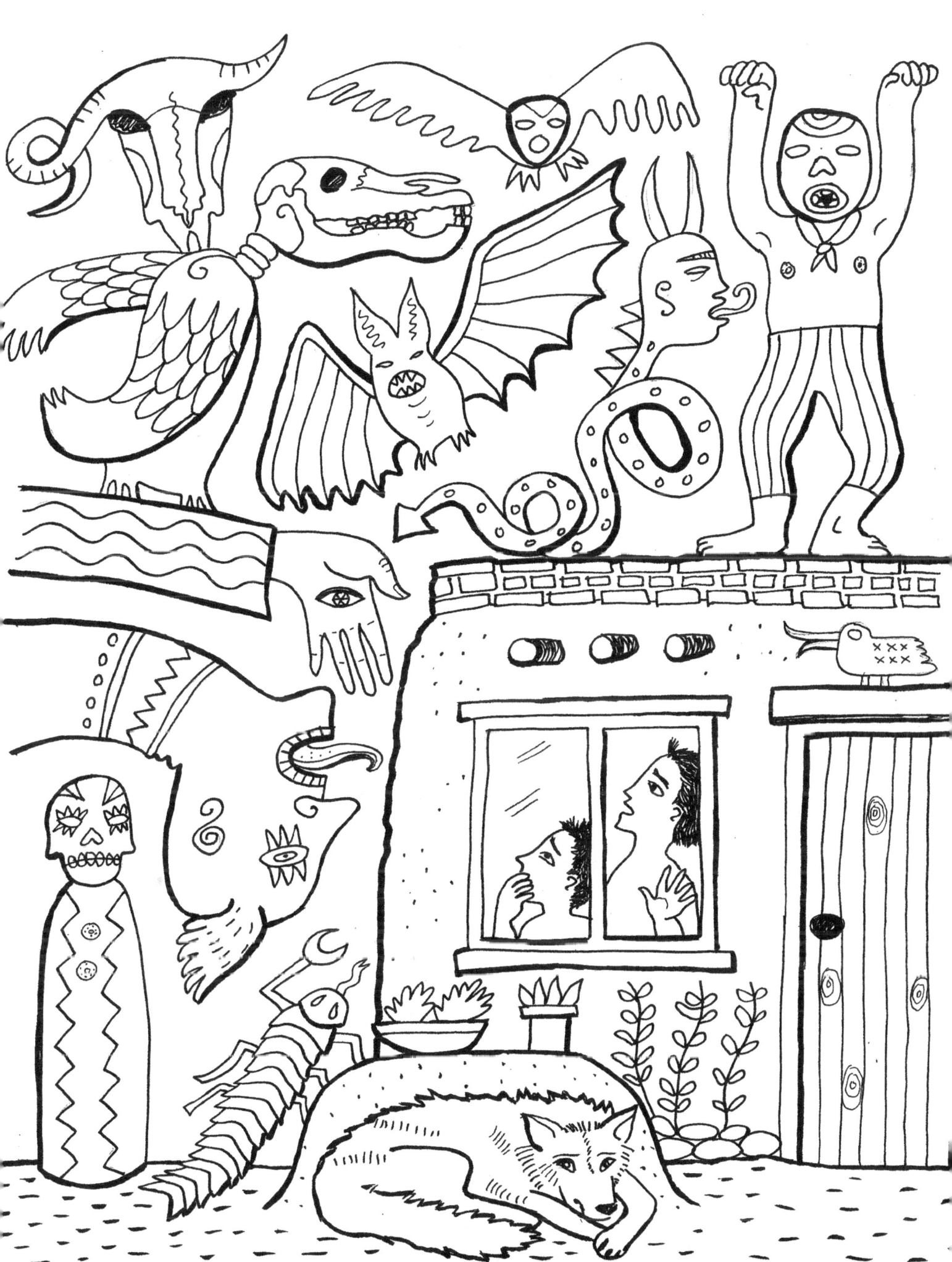

Joel Nakamura

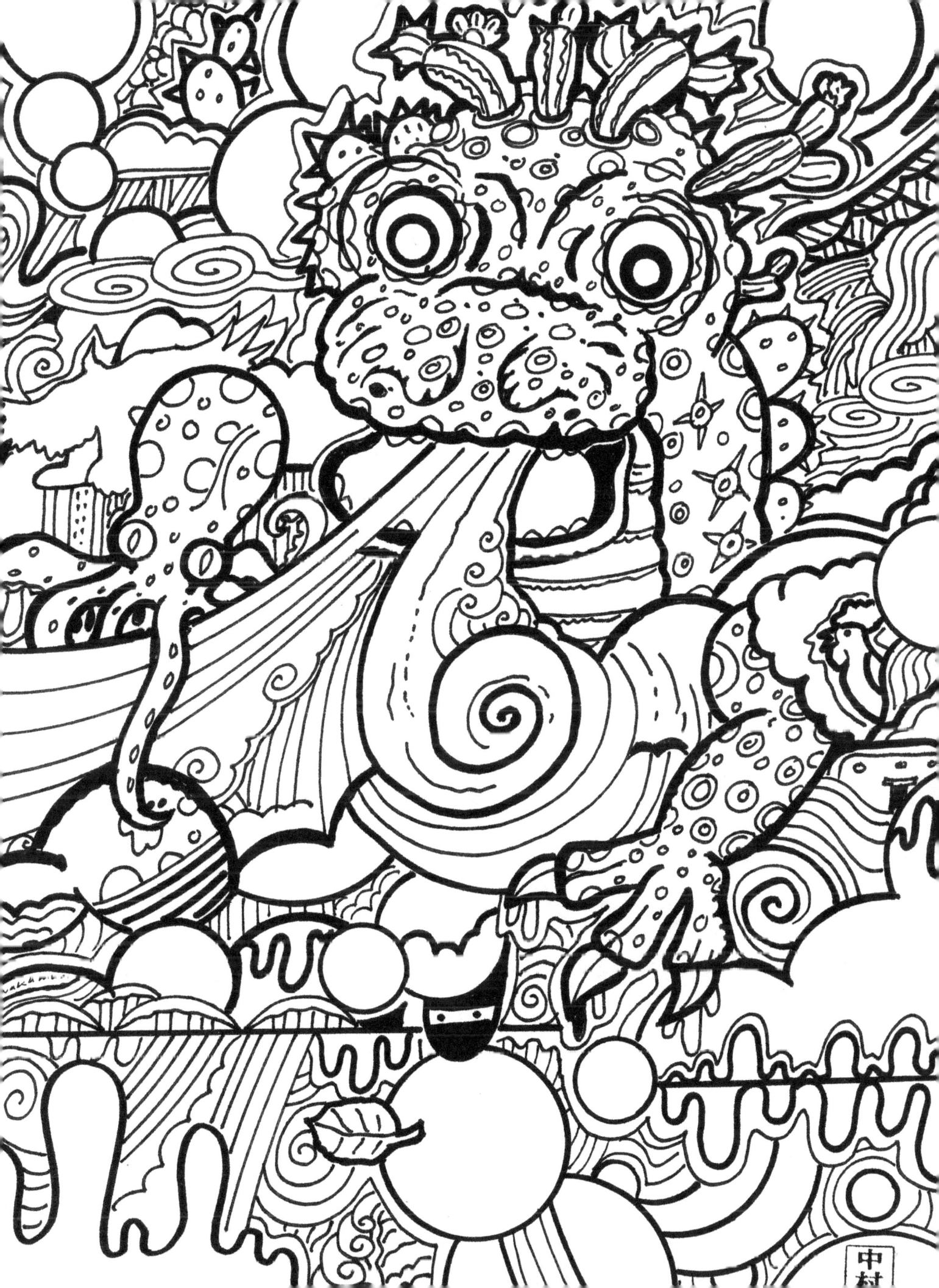

Shakti Kroopkin

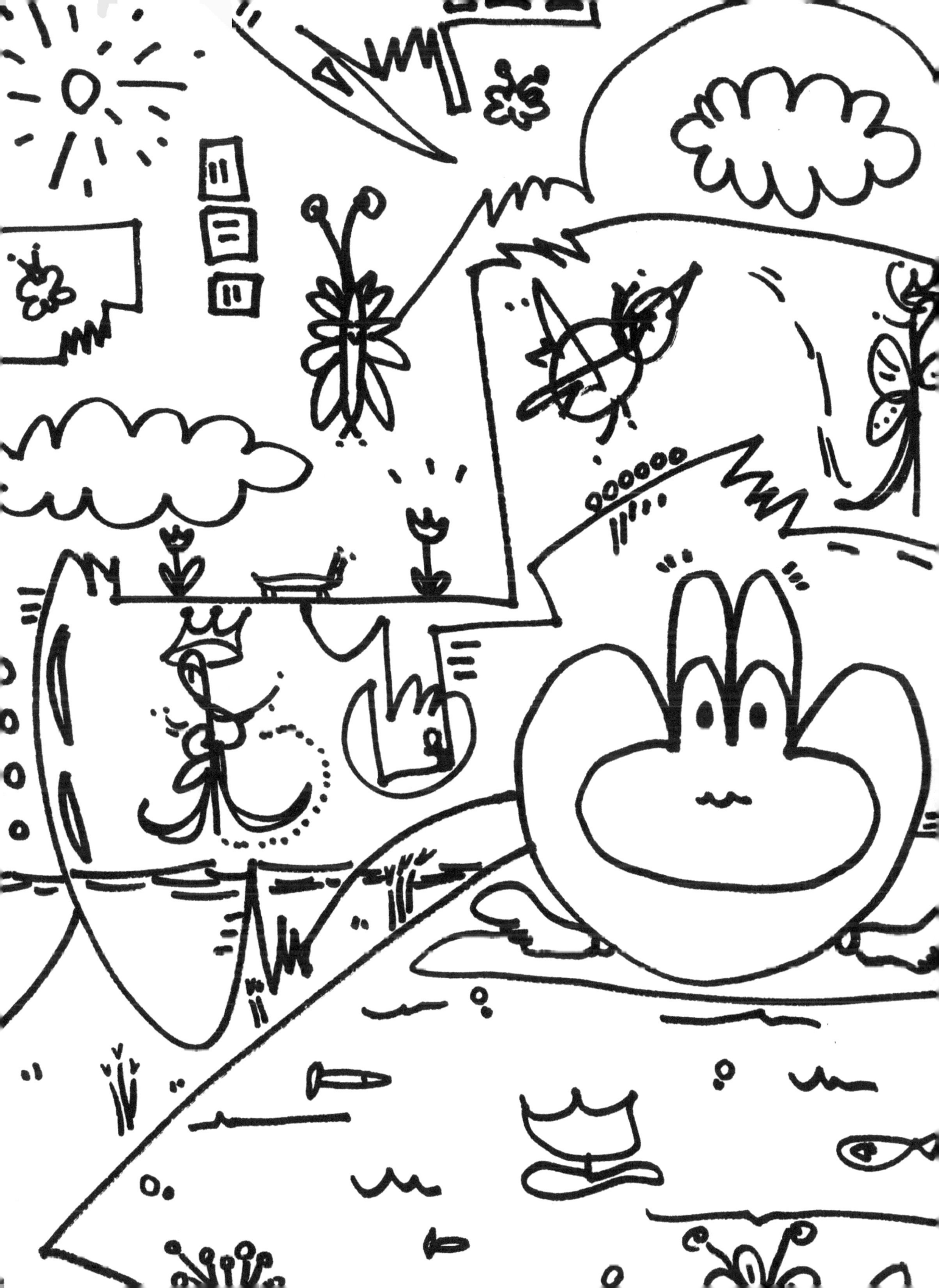

Yubi Kim

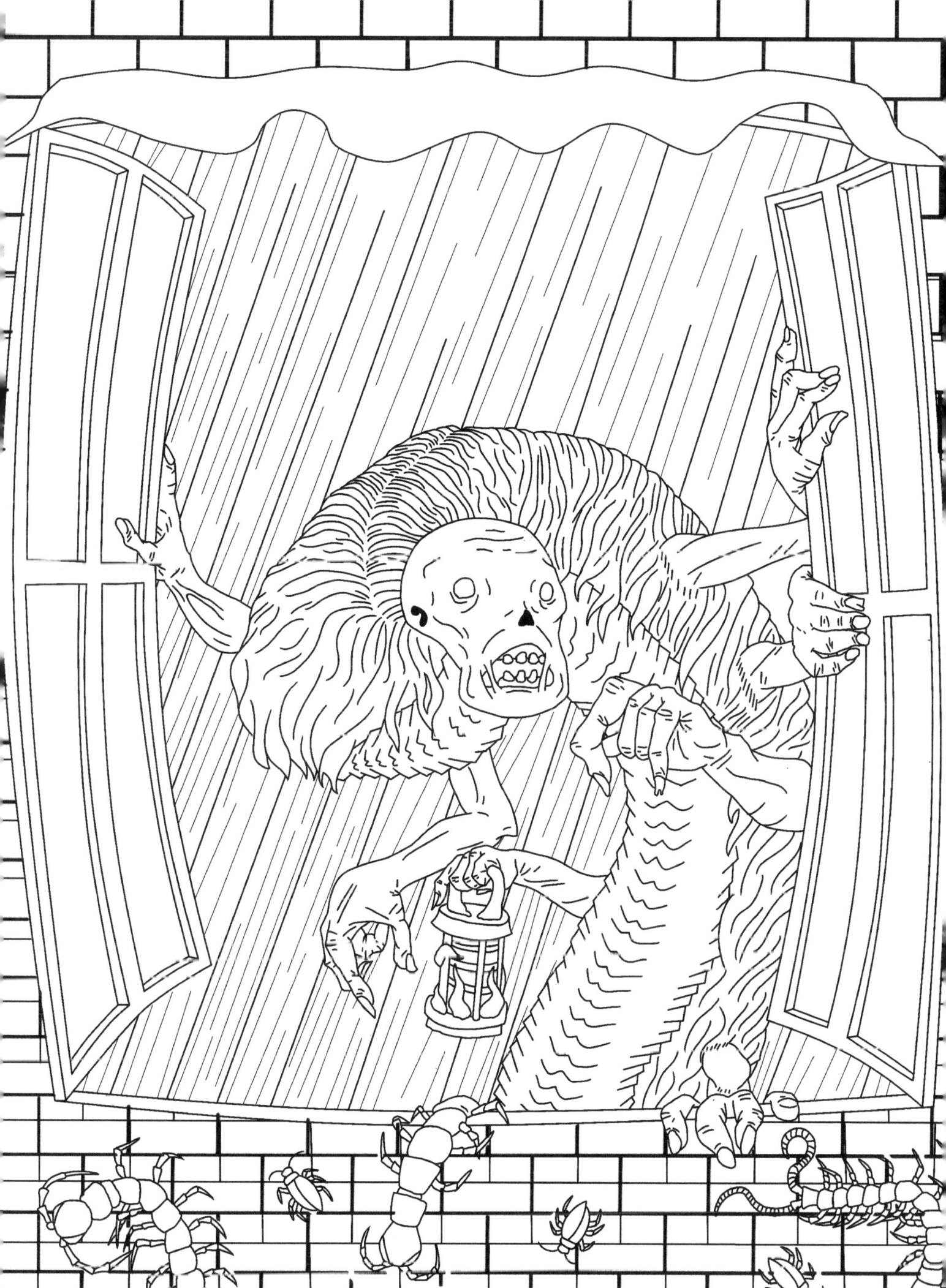

Raina Wellman

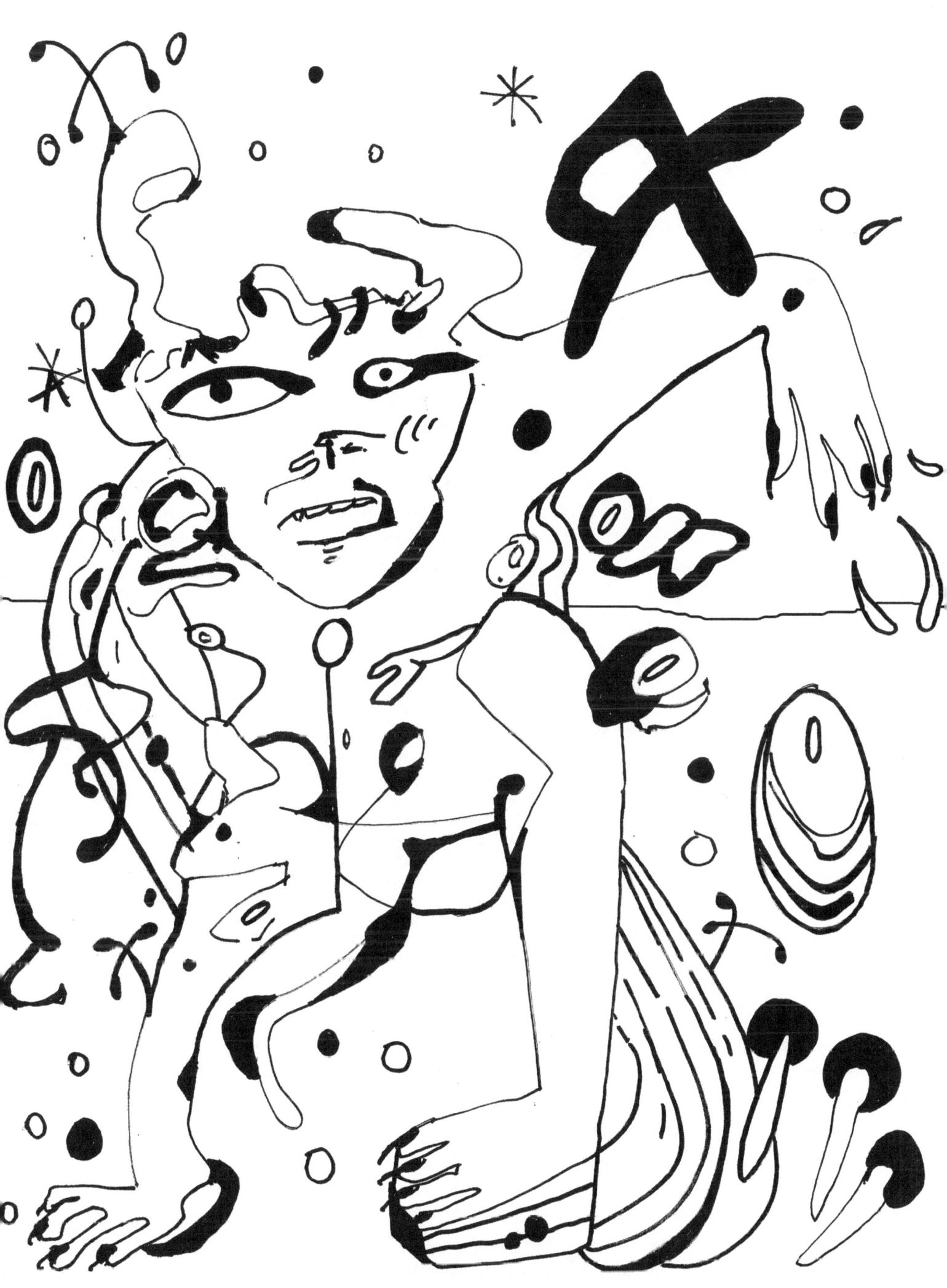

Larry Bob Phillips

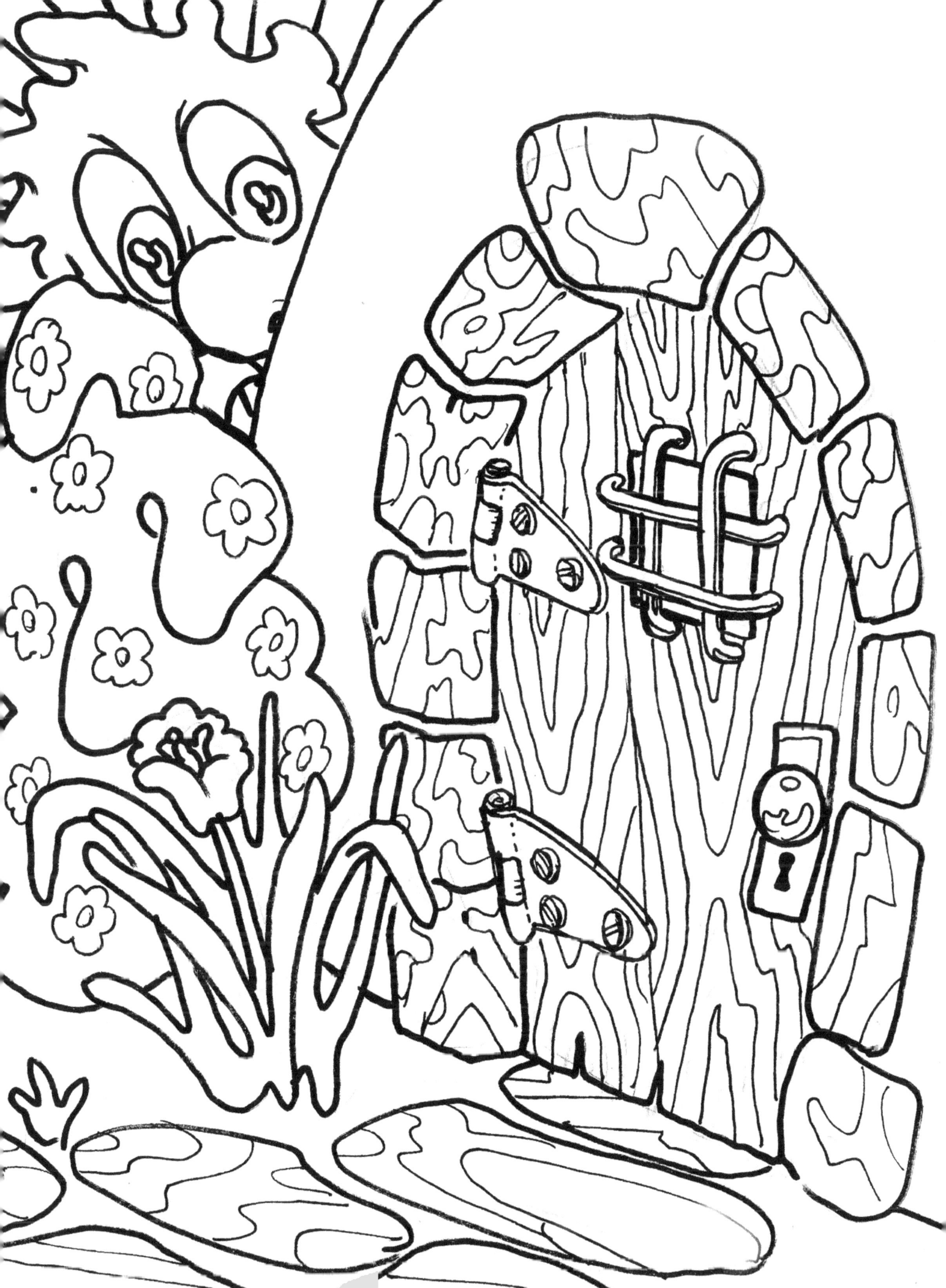

Linda Swanson

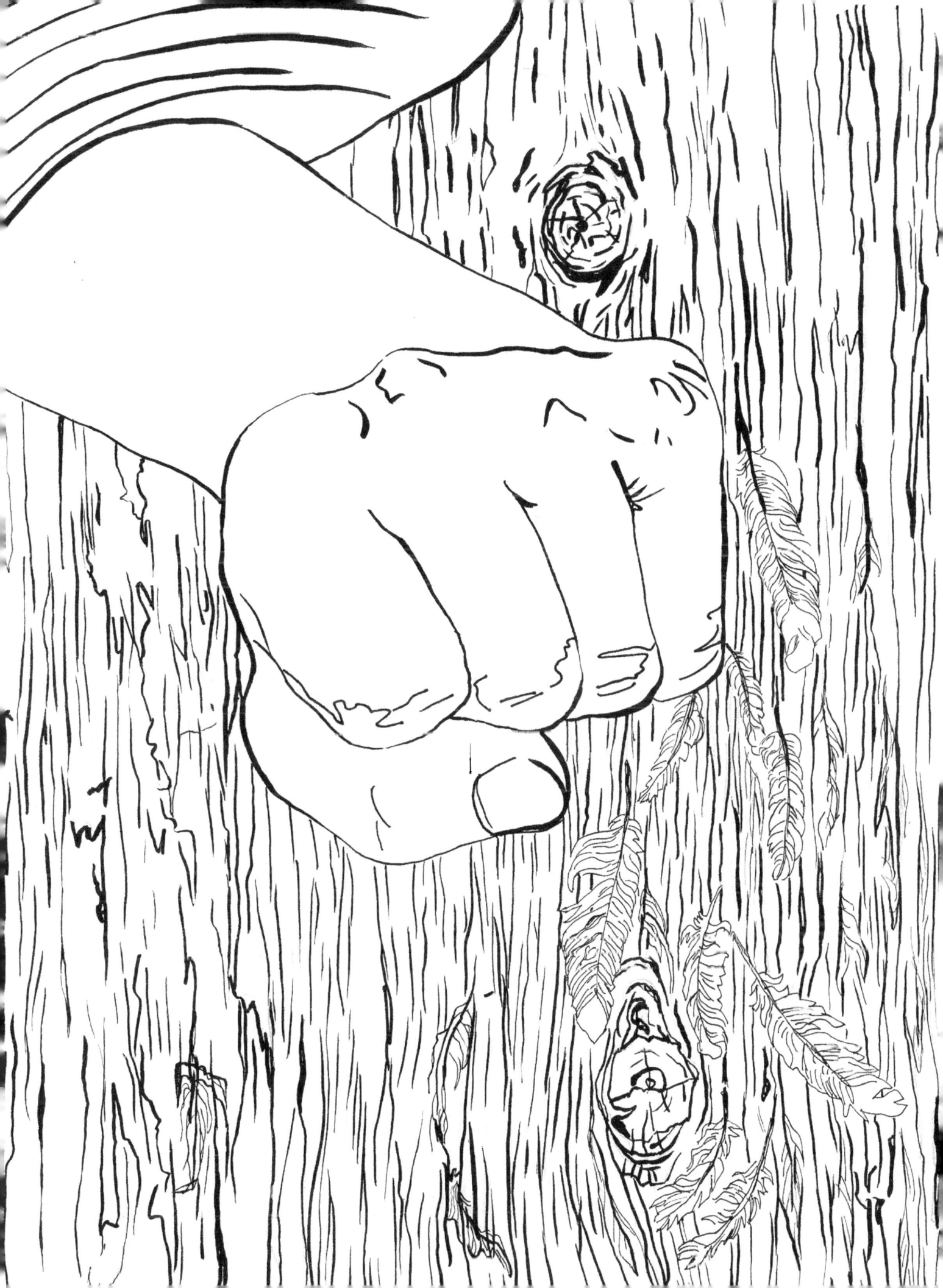

Jamison Chas Banks

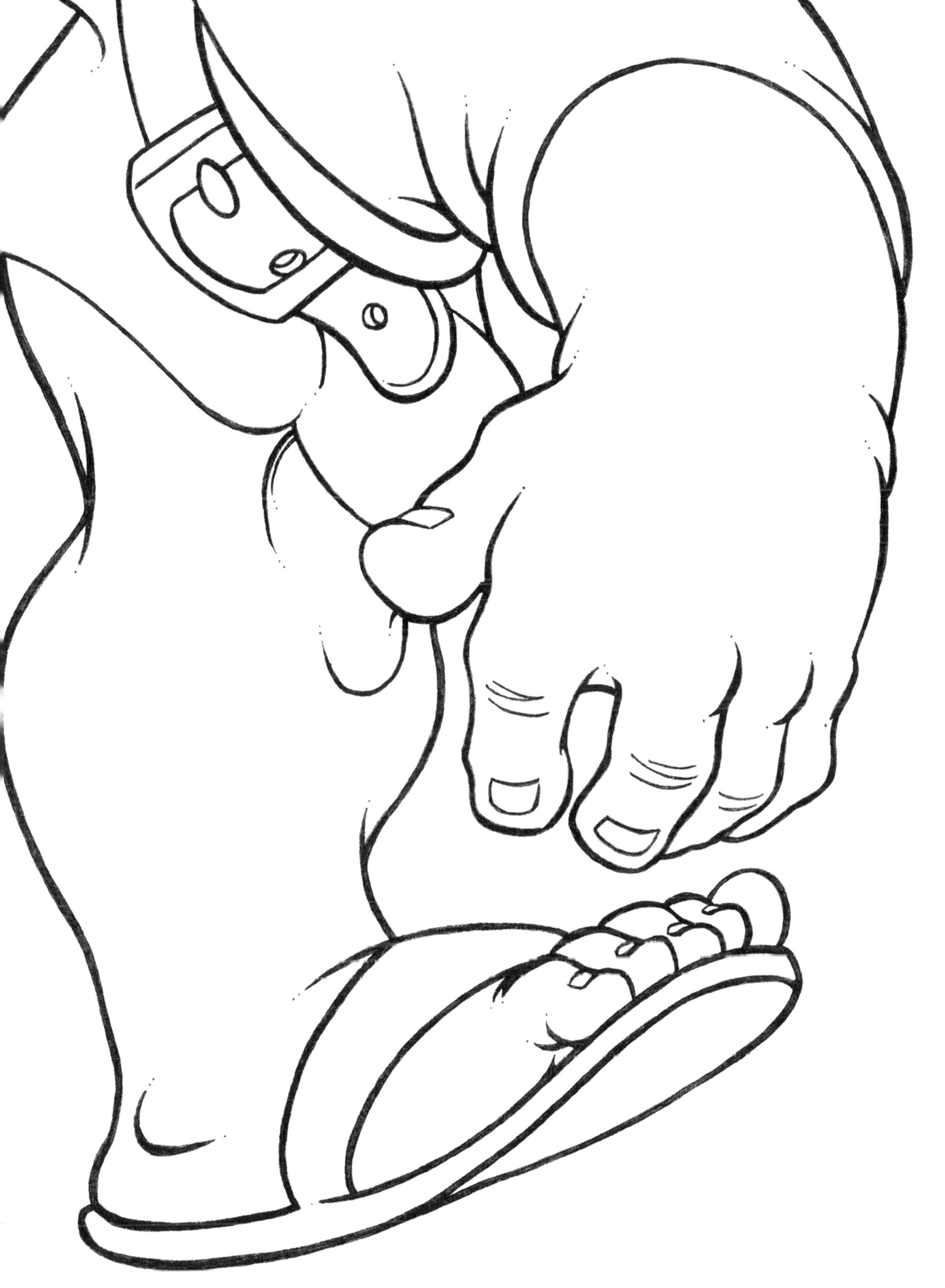

Hans Harland-Hue

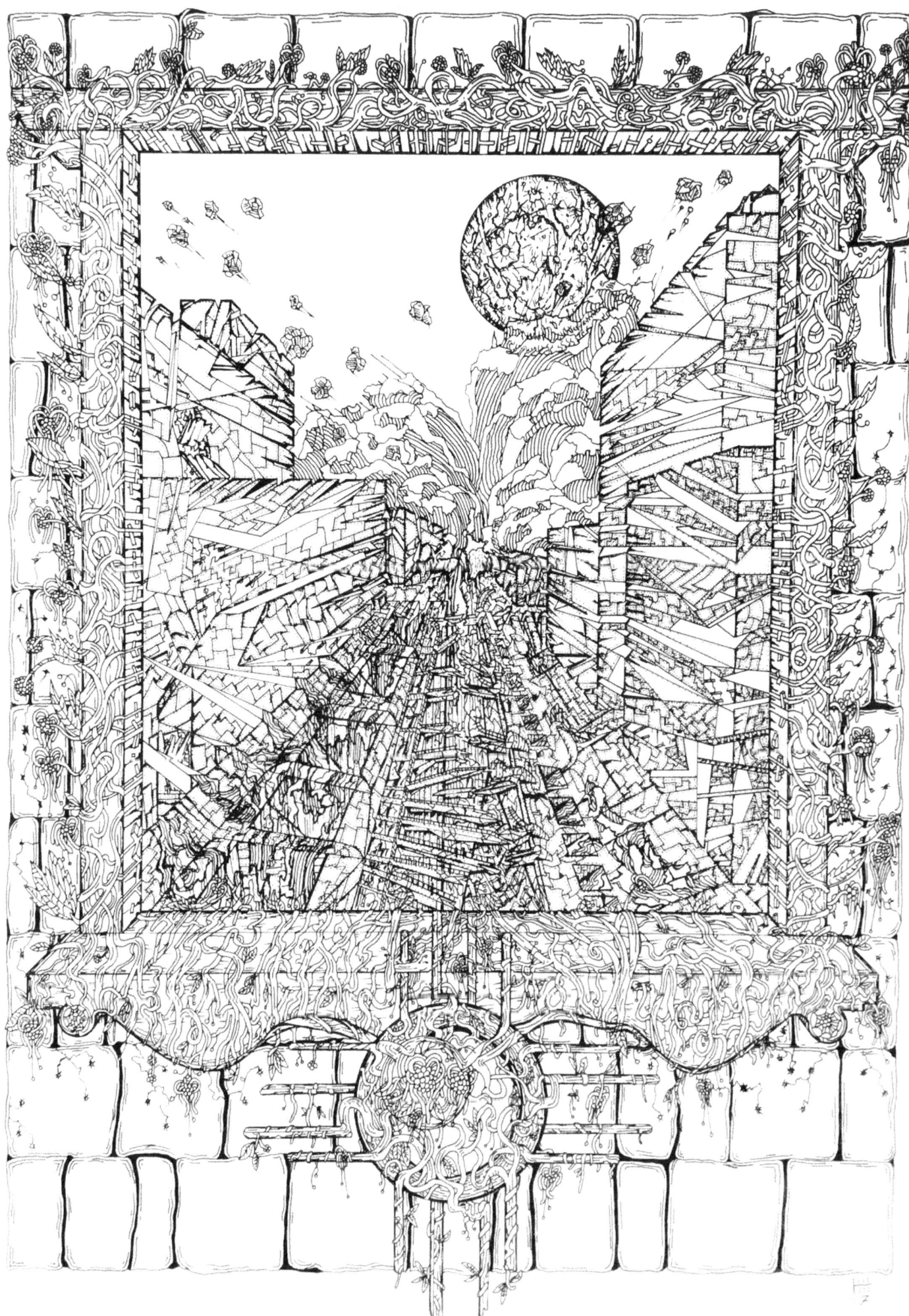

Melody Sumner Carnahan has twelve books in print and over forty short works published in periodicals and anthologies, including *City Lights Review, Leonardo Music Journal, THE Magazine, At a Distance* (MIT), *The Closets of Time* (Mercury Press), and *Permission to Speak* (Teksteditions). Her fiction also finds form off-the-page as stories, lyrics, and prose for recordings, installations, video, and performance. Acknowledgements have come from the NEA, New American Radio, CBC in Canada, NTT/ICC in Tokyo, and ABC in Australia, where she was Creative Media Arts Fellow 2000. Carnahan's book w/ audio CD, *The Time Is Now*, received an Independent Publisher Book Award in Audiofiction. A Carnahan collaboration with artist Michael Sumner, *One Inch Equals Twenty-Five Miles*, was presented live and on CD by the Out of Context ensemble, and won an Eric Hoffer Book Award. Carnahan's novel, *Only a Messenger* (Quadrants Series) was awarded an IPPY Bronze Medal. Her fourth story collection, *You Are Not Asleep*, was released by Teksteditions, Canada, 2014. *Twice Though the Maze*, the latest collaboration with Michael Sumner, was exhibited at Phil Space in 2016. See: www.sumnercarnahan.org

Jamie Figueroa holds an MFA in Creative Writing from The Institute of American Indian Arts in Santa Fe, New Mexico. Her poetry and prose have been published in various literary journals including *Epoch, Catapult, Hinchas de Poesia, Yellow Medicine Review, Flash: International, Eleven Eleven, Sin Fronteras*, and others. Jamie has taught students ranging from middle school to graduate school. She has been involved with the nonprofits Little Globe, El Otro Lado, The Cut+Paste Society, and the Identity Project, organizations where art and creative practice merge with social activism. Jamie is represented by the literary agency Janklow and Nesbit Associates.

Folklorist, creative writer and native New Mexican **Nasario García** has published numerous award winning books about Hispanic folklore and the oral history of northern New Mexico, including *Grandma's Santo on Its Head / El santo patas arriba de mi abuelita: Stories of Days Gone By in Hispanic Villages of New Mexico / Cuentos de días gloriosos en pueblitos hispanos de Nuevo México, Grandma Lale's Tamales: A Christmas Story, Grandpa Lolo's Navajo Saddle Blanket: La tilma de Abuelito Lolo, Grandpa Lolo's Matanza: A New Mexico Tradition*, and *Hoe, Heaven, and Hell: My Boyhood in Rural New Mexico*. Garcia currently lives in Santa Fe, New Mexico, with his wife Janice.

Joe Hayes is the premier storyteller of New Mexico and the Southwest. He is an award-winning author of nearly 30 books for young readers, many in both English and Spanish. His books have received the Arizona Young Readers Award, two Land of Enchantment Children's Book Awards, and the Texas Bluebonnet Award. His first book, *The Day It Snowed Tortillas*, has been in print for 35 years and has become a regional classic. His most recent title, *Grandpa's Hal-a-loo-yah Hambone*, was chosen by the editors of *School Library Journal* as one of the best picture books published in 2016. Joe was designated a New Mexico Eminent Scholar by the New Mexico Commission on Higher Learning and received the New Mexico Governor's Award for Excellence in the Arts. Joe's storytelling sessions at the Wheelwright Museum are a Santa Fe summer tradition. A whole generation of Santa Fe children grew up listening to Joe's stories and are now bringing their own sons and daughters to Museum Hill to hear his tales.

Lily Hoang is the author of five books, including *A Bestiary* (winner of the inaugural Cleveland State University Poetry Center's Nonfiction Contest) and *Changing* (recipient of a PEN Open Books Award). With Blake Butler, she edited *30 Under 30*, and with Joshua Marie Wilkinson, she edited *The Force of What's Possible: Writers on Accessibility and the Avant Garde*. She formerly taught in the MFA program at New Mexico State University, where she was prose editor of *Puerto del Sol*. Honored as a Distinguished Visiting Writer at Cornell College, Hoang currently teaches at University of California San Diego.

....

Housed in a retrofitted aluminum step van, the **Axle Contemporary** mobile gallery brings contemporary art from New Mexico artists to appreciative audiences throughout Santa Fe, Northern New Mexico, and beyond. Axle's innovative outreach program intersects disciplines and encourages and promotes experimental and creative approaches to art-making and presentation. Founded in 2010 by artists Mathhew Chase-Daniel and Jerry Wellman, Axle reaches a diverse community in the places where they live and work: City streets, grocery stores, parking lots, schools, restaurants, city parks, and more. Axle Contemporary Press has published fourteen books that celebrate, promote, and sustain interest and innovation in the arts.

ARTIST INDEX

www.ingramcontent.com/pod-product-compliance
Lightning Source LLC
Chambersburg PA
CBHW080915170526
45158CB00008B/2123